EXPRESSIVE KAVANNAH
Creativity, Meaning and Healing

Edna Miron-Wapner

Dear Sally,
My soul sister
Hoping to share
many more adventures.
Love, E

"Tree of Life"

Dedication

To *Ima*, my Grandma Rela, who bequeathed me her voice
and the joy of singing, a way to keep her alive in me

Reflections on Expressive Kavannah

"When I first heard about Edna Miron-Wapner's commitment to exploring the relationship between artistic expression and Kavannah many years ago, I strongly encouraged her to follow this passion which I felt would make an important contribution to many realms of human experience. This vision has been realized with the publication of Expressive Kavannah: Creativity, Meaning and Healing. The book offers an erudite and rich educational description of Kavannah within Jewish tradition while modeling how artistic expression and reflection can be used to enhance prayer and contemplative practice in all aspects of religious and spiritual experience."

Shaun McNiff, author of <u>Imagination in Action</u>, <u>Trust the Process: An Artists Guide to Letting Go</u>, <u>Art Heals</u>, <u>Art as Medicine</u>, and many other internationally acclaimed books

"Edna Miron-Wapner has been diligently leading a life of Jewish creativity for decades. Not only is her own calligraphic painting a form of prayer, but she has created a pathway into the Torah and through the Jewish calendar via art making and has shared it with countless students. With the publication of Expressive Kavannah she is sharing the roadmap with all of us. Movement, poetry and painting are the ingredients she uses to leaven the texts, helping to create a Judaism that is available to all. Edna brings a deeply feminine sensibility to her work that nourishes and heals the soul."

Pat B. Allen, author of <u>Art is a Way of Knowing</u> and <u>Art is a Spiritual Path</u>

"Edna Miron Wapner's 'Expressive Kavannah' has rewarded me with surprising self-expression through fresh engagement with sacred text, time, and ritual. In her writing she harvests years of facilitating such discovery and guides facilitators on how to open up the intuitive channels of spiritual creativity and connection."

Rabbi Elie Spitz, author of <u>Does the Soul Survive?</u> and <u>Increasing Wholeness</u>

"Expressive Kavannah is an empowering multi-modality that supports reflection, growth, creativity, learning, and healing. For over 25 years, Edna has lead many workshops for the graduate students and professionals studying in my seminars; each time challenging and opening up the participants to new perspectives within themselves in dialogue with our tradition and texts. Edna creates the sacred space to support their exploration and taking risks. Expressive Kavannah is powerful and an inspiring gift that Edna has brought to Jewish Education!"

Sally Klein-Katz, Jewish Educator

TABLE OF CONTENTS

PROLOGUE
GODLINESS-ELOHUT

*"The roots of ultimate insights are found, on the level of wonder
and radical amazement, in the depth of awe, in our sensitivity to the
mystery, in our awareness of the ineffable. It is the level on which the
great things happen to the soul, where unique insights of art, religion
and philosophy come into being. It is not from experience but 'from
our inability to experience' what is given to the mind that certainty of
the realness of God is derived. Our certainty is the result of wonder
and radical amazement, of awe before the mystery and meaning of
the totality of life beyond rational discerning. Faith is the 'response' to
the mystery…such a response is a sign of man's essential dignity. It
is an act of spiritual ecstasy."*

Rabbi Abraham Joshua Heschel's concept of radical amazement from his book <u>God in Search of Man: A Philosophy of Judaism</u> touches me deeply and informs my attitude to the divine. In writing this book I struggled with the question of how to explain my use of the term God and the numerous names we Jews use in an attempt to express the ineffable. I do not claim to know God, but I am comfortable as a progressive, eclectic Jew with the use of traditional God language.

Throughout this book I use the word God, or one of the many other names – *HaShem*, literally "the Name", *Shechinah*, Creator, or the Divine – all to invoke a transcendent experience. As a woman, I especially gravitate to the concept of God's feminine presence, the *Shechinah*, within the divine unity. It is a sense of "unknowing" knowing presence I feel in my heart and soul beyond normal perception. I seek as an artist to fuse my spiritual inclinations with my creative impulse. Engaging in artistic expression, I feel a connection to a universal creative source.

In <u>The Book of Blessings, a Jewish Prayer Book</u>, poet Dr. Marcia Falk replaces traditional masculine terminology for God, such as Lord or King, with what she calls "new images for divinity", as in her translation of the central Jewish prayer, the *Shema*: "Hear O Israel – The divine abounds everywhere and dwells in everything; the many are One".

As a spiritual artist, I am moved and awed by nature where I experience the transcendent most vividly. The artistry of the trees with their branches reaching for the heavens, luminous skies, ethereal sunsets and atmospheric perspective of mountains nurture my soul.

When in the midst of artwork in my studio, I often feel a divine presence as I enter a state of flow and a heightened sense of reality. My emotions come alive in the vibrant force of the brushstrokes and the flowing energy of the inks. I feel the power of the moment. I trust in the process. An intuitive and spontaneous creation is born. Powerful healing, *tikkun*, which affects me body and soul, is channeled through this process. I feel at one with brush, ink and paper.

Expressive Kavannah is an artistic, contemplative and therapeutic practice. I am interested in the qualities and acts of Godliness rather than in philosophical or religious discourse about God.

"Celebration"

I strive to offer others a glimpse of the divinity within each of us, human beings created in the image of God. An influential teacher, Rabbi Harold Schulweis, of blessed memory, proposes "a shift, from noun to verb, from subject to predicate, from God as a person to Godliness, in Hebrew 'Elohut.' Not the qualities of divinity but the divinity of the qualities are essential to belief."

In my daily meditation I embrace the sense of entering into a safe, sacred space. I aspire to empty my mind of extraneous thoughts and sensations to reach a place of stillness. Whether I have focused my meditations on mindfulness, or a seed thought from a prayer or the Torah, I emerge in serenity and clarity to close with a practice of gratitude for the myriad blessings of my life.

Similarly, when I engage in the communal experience of prayer, blessing, chanting and singing, I become part of the landscape of prayer, uplifted and supported by a chorus of voices of which mine is one. Expressing the words of the prayers with kavannah, becomes a way of communicating with a higher realm to bring about a sense of oneness and belonging.

Expressive Kavannah works with others to unlock our innate creativity. I use my personal experience of meditation and prayer, of study and struggle to offer a framework to apprehend the Godliness of your own qualities. I direct my students, truly my fellow spiritual seekers, to focus, as I too do, on pursuing a path out of our routine self-centered domain— to one embracing the basic Jewish values of kavannah "focused intention", mitzvah "selfless act", and tikkun olam "repair of the world". Transformation begins to take place in the readiness to question our purpose and responsibility in the grand scheme of existence. I strive to engender and nourish a quiet, safe sacred space where each one is invited to create for the sake of creating, to encounter the unknown and raise awareness and consciousness of godliness at work in their lives.

My mentor Dr. Pat Allen affirms "we create our spiritual connection by attending to the soul. Spirit enters when soul has made the place ready. Soul is basic, everyday...it is everything to do with daily life. When we cultivate soul... we see spirit and feel it, a sense of awe and reverence in many different situations."

1

MY JOURNEY

Images, my first exhibition of spiritual art, shown at the Magnes Museum in Berkeley, California in 1992, first conceptualized "Art as *Tikkun*: Healing and Transformation". I boldly stated, "I am a Jewish transformative artist. The intention, *kavannah*, is to heal the mind, body and spirit of the artist – a personal repair, *tikkun*, through the creative process. Furthermore, I hope to involve the receptive viewer in the universal call of Jewish tradition, repair and heal the world, *tikkun olam*, through the art itself. In my quest for meaning rather than just beauty in my art, I fulfill a deep personal need for purpose." Crucial to my artistic and pedagogic development, I had recognized the therapeutic effect of the creative act. My own spiritual and artistic journey is the path that led me to develop Expressive Kavannah. I feel passionate to share this experience which is so powerful for me.

My own exploration started in Canada and intuitively brought me to Jerusalem. This move created two important and formative aspects of healing, *tikkunim*, in my life. Jerusalem remains my home 40 years later, a place of ethereal light, spirituality and beauty. Here I feel centered and embraced. Here my life blossomed and flourished creating family, developing friends and community and owning my Jewish identity. Although I grew up in an artistic home in Montreal, that was never my interest or inclination. I can only surmise that Jerusalem's special beauty, mingling divine and mundane, allowed the artist within to emerge, inspiring me to master Hebrew calligraphy, an echo of my history and connection to this land. Essentially, this was the beginning of my journey.

Shortly after I resettled in Jerusalem, my father died suddenly in Canada. I was overwhelmed with grief. I instinctively surrendered to the healing power of the creative process.

Edna in the studio

Each piece emanated from an inner sanctuary through which pain, anger, joy and love are given tangible expression and form. My emotions came alive in the vibrant force of the brushstrokes and flowing energy of the inks – an intuitive and spontaneous creation. Healing was taking place within. I was in intense flow. Completely absorbed, I felt at one with brush, ink and paper. I found a place of comfort and transformation. I felt blessed by this intense personal experience where I found healing and gained clarity. My *kavannah*, focused intentionality, in the artistic process enabled healing which in turn strengthened my *kavannah*.

Today, Jewish practice and learning are the foundation of my path both as a Jewish spiritual artist and a facilitator of Expressive Kavannah. Spirituality denotes the search for meaning, connection and purpose in life. It is experienced as a sense of unknowing knowing in heart and soul, a presence beyond. I experience *Shechinah*, the feminine aspect of God, guiding me to a higher state of consciousness – oneness, union, peace – in meditation, in prayer, in creativity and in nature. I need courage and faith in myself. My personal spiritual journey brings me to a place of flow from which inspiration and creation spring forth spontaneously. I strive to develop my intuition and foster a non-judgmental self-awareness. I engage with process, the unfolding, which holds the secret of the meaning. I allow the end product to always be a surprise engaging me in intense introspection. It is essential I not judge, as my subconscious does not always present me with beauty, yet always cries out for my attention. My *kavannah* to heal, intuitive and experiential, weaves together my spirituality and creativity to elevate and enhance the understanding of my inner life.

The methodology of Expressive Kavannah evolved from my studies and research, combined with my experiences in Judaism, the arts, expressive arts therapy and meditation techniques. As a rich spiritual model for integration of the arts, Expressive Kavannah provides a profound educational and therapeutic experience and supportive atmosphere of others' personal growth and self-awareness. It is a synthesis made possible by the support and trust my teachers and colleagues instilled in me to pursue my own path.

As Jews, and particularly in Israel, we live according to a Jewish calendar. Expressive Kavannah follows the Jewish yearly holiday cycle: Shabbat, our weekly day of rest from Creation, with communal prayer services and recitation and study of Torah portions; and festive annual holidays, each adding an abundance of ritual, special blessings and study opportunities. Each different observance imparts a personal aspect within the collective atmosphere, in turn influencing the community as a whole. As I continue to develop and refine Expressive Kavannah I strive to create a context in which the individual can experience and explore the Jewish cycle of celebration in a personal, reflective and meaningful fashion. In so doing, each participant prepares personally to bring their own *kavannah* to the communal experience.

The goal of this book is to facilitate accessing your unique creativity, to empower you through an inner journey. Everyone is inherently creative, each made in God's image. Expressive Kavannah is a spiritual, spontaneous, learning and teaching model that enables personal exploration through writing, movement, voice and image-making in a supportive group environment. No experience is required in the arts or Judaism. I guide meditation and study to facilitate experimentation in a personal, reflective and meaningful way. You are invited to experiment with your creativity; to let go; to engage in spontaneous creations; to be more intuitive; to simply enjoy the process; and finally, to trust the process in accessing purpose and meaning. As others in the group experience their own processes, a group spirit emerges as a support for the exploration. That knowledge and experience can enhance and transform many aspects of your life.

I trust this book is a useful learning, teaching and therapeutic tool for young adults and adults alike in the heterodox and orthodox communities in the Diaspora and Israel: rabbis, educators, group leaders and students. In it you will learn the background and application of Expressive Kavannah. I share my own journey and exploration that brought me to develop the methodology and techniques. I explain the methodology as well as offer instructions and suggestions for the facilitator. Throughout the book, prayers, blessings, Torah portions and holiday observances take on creative and personal interpretations to illustrate the concepts. Although my model is inspired and based on Jewish tradition, I feel it carries a universal message. I am confident that with appropriate cultural and religious modifications similar positive impact can be achieved. Expressive Kavannah awakens creativity by enabling the imagination to transform familiar narratives and practices into personal, meaningful expressions. You will be creating spontaneous interpretation, *midrash*, as you engage the spirit artfully!

$$\boxed{2}$$

THE CONCEPT OF KAVANNAH

Kavannah – from the Hebrew root *lekaven,* to direct – has a number of important connotations. At various times, over the centuries, it has been defined as intention, direction, focus, concentration, attention, devotion, and even meditation. It means all of these, and more, the sum being greater than its parts. Originally, *kavannah* is referred to as both the mindset of humility for performing Jewish rituals and the practice of Jewish meditation to attain closeness with God.

Kavannah in Prayer

Prayer is one way of communicating with God. Reading or reciting from a prayer book is only one aspect, as my teacher and Rabbi Levi Weiman-Kelman calls it the *p'shat,* the basic level. More important is our attitude and the introspection it provides. *Kavannah* implies a mind free from other thoughts, that you know and understand the content of your praying and reflect on its meaning. *Kavannah* is the Jew's sense of standing in the presence of God and offering the words with sincerity, purity and humility, directing hearts to heaven. *Kavannah* in prayer lets the words direct your consciousness and vice versa. The Talmud teaches "One who prays must direct his eyes downward and his heart on high".

The Hebrew root ברך forms the words *baruch* and *bracha,* bless and blessing. The same letters form the word *berech,* meaning knee, alluding to the practice of bending one's knees or bowing in prayer. This same root also forms the word *brecha,* pool of water,

source of all life. We bend expressing a sense of humility. Our intention is focused. Our attitude is gratitude. We desire to receive the
blessings in our lives. Blessings transform us, and we transform the
blessings in a reciprocal dance of meaning.

A biblical example of *kavannah* is evident in Moses' prayer for
Miriam in *Baha'alotecha* (Numbers 12:13): "Please God, Heal Her
Now, *El Na Refah Na La*". A sincere and spontaneous cry from the
heart, a direct plea to God, to which an immediate response follows –
God heals Miriam.

Hannah's prayer in Samuel I 1:12-15 is similar: "as she continued praying before the Lord, Eli the priest noticed her mouth. Now
Hannah spoke in her heart; only her lips moved, but her voice was
not heard...I poured out my soul before the Lord." Hannah's silent
prayer was a prayer from the heart, poured out with *kavannah*, a
personal moment between Hannah and her God.

In the rabbinic tradition, the *Gemara* (*Berakhot* 31a) teaches
that one must have proper intentions during prayers. "When a man
prays, he should direct his heart to heaven. A reminder of this is
found in Psalms 10:17 (*Tehillim*), 'You will direct their heart, and you
will cause their ear to listen'..."

In the *Shulchan Arukh* (101:1) we find: "One who prays
should concentrate for ALL of the *brachot.*"

The *Rambam* (Maimonides 1135-1204), writes in the
Guide for the Perplexed (4:15-16): "What role does *kavannat ha-
lev* (intention of the heart) play? Any *tefilah*, prayer, which lacks *kavannat ha-lev* is NOT a *tefilah.*"

The Kabbalistic tradition sets a new ideal for the concept of
kavannah with a wider interpretation of self-directness, mental effort
or will power. In *Essential Kabbalah*, world-renowned scholar Daniel
Matt defines *kavannah* as "a meditative intention directed to a particular word of prayer, divine name or divine quality." *Kavannah*, considered a state of higher consciousness, then becomes the essence of

the transcendent experience, not just a feature of the formal prayer service.

Lastly, Abraham Joshua Heschel (1907-1972), a leading scholar of Jewish thought in the 20th century, states: "*Kavannah* is the direction to God." It is an act of love – "thou shalt love... with all thy heart, and with all thy soul and with all thy might" (Deuteronomy 6:5-6). Love of God is an awareness that has its own intrinsic meaning and purpose. Heschel brings God and therefore *kavannah* into daily modern life: "Right living is a way to right thinking. The way to *kavannah* is through the *mitzvah,* selfless act; the way of faith is a way of living." Accepting the presence of God in our lives is a commitment to integrate Him into our whole being in order to transform us. Understanding and development of my own *kavannah* grew out of positive synagogue experiences that led to the desire to undertake Jewish learning. Simultaneously, I actively integrated these mystical concepts of *kavannah, mitzvah* and *tikkun olam* with art as a transformative process. *Tikkun* literally translates as repair, rectification or healing. Through our *kavannah* and *mitzvot* we restore harmony and balance in the world. Today facing myriad ecological crises we learn that our actions, lifestyles and consumer decisions may have profound consequences. Each small selfless act performed with the intention of healing the planet reinforces humanity's collective efforts and transforms our own behavior.

For 25 years Kehilat Kol Haneshama in Jerusalem has been my spiritual home. Rabbi Levi Weiman-Kelman's service gave my personal Jewish meditation practice depth and a new place to express itself. Rabbi Levi refers to prayer as playing jazz. Sometimes, I need to blend my voice in chanting with the community; sometimes I hum the *niggun,* wordless melody; and I also sit in silent meditation in the "landscape of prayer". Physically being immersed in a place where others are engaged in spiritual pursuits supports my own.

The liturgical melodies are a way to focus as my voice is a

powerful conduit for my *kavannah* in prayer. When I sing, I feel connected to my remarkable grandmother, Rela, known universally with great affection as *Ima*, Mother, an opera singer and gynecologist. *Ima* died just four months after my first child Gabriel was born in 1984. She seemed to take it as a sign to let go of a great long life well lived. Most of my life, I had no aptitude for music or singing. Surprisingly, one day while singing to Gabriel, a new voice burst forth. Perhaps *Ima* bequeathed me her voice. What I do know is that each time I let my voice flow I sense her alive in me.

The prayers became a way of communicating with a higher realm to bring about oneness, a sense of belonging. Expressing the words of the prayers with *kavannah*, intention and sincerity, makes these personal and meaningful to me. I am humbled by sensing and directing myself to a world beyond my own.

Kavannah in Meditation

Meditation has a long history in Jewish tradition from medieval times. Kabbalists, the Jewish mystics from medieval Spain and later in Safed, wrote about it extensively and experimented with a variety of techniques to ascend to heavenly realms. Revived by Hasidism in Eastern Europe, only to virtually disappear from popular practice due to the dominance of rational normative Judaism. Today, it has reemerged all across the spectrum of Jewish practice, alongside growing interest generally in Jewish mysticism, *Kabbalah*. A variety of meditation practices are being taught freely and widely. "One would have to take a deep plunge into the Jewish mind...into the intricacies of the *Kabbalah*, which still remains psychologically unexplored," states renowned psychologist Carl Jung.

All with the same main goal of attaining closeness to God, there are three distinct Hebrew words for the act of meditation: *kavannah/kavannot, hitbonenut and hitbodedut.* All are in the reflexive form indicating reciprocal relationships. While the techniques may vary, all practices share a common aspect, each is utilized with focused intention, *kavannah.*

Kavannah itself is the most widely accepted word for meditation in mystical Jewish literature. It is derived from the Hebrew word *kaven*, to direct, therefore *kavannah* meditation practice refers to techniques of directed consciousness.

Hitbonenut derives from the root word *bin* (or *lehavin*), which has many related derivatives including *binah*, understanding, and *bonen*, to perceive or observe. *Hitbonenut* meditation strives to go penetrate deeply into oneself, observing to gain insight and achieve understanding.

Hitbodedut is from the root word *boded*, alone. Its reflexive form literally means being alone/secluded with oneself, and refers to isolating oneself to clear the mind of outside sensations, attain a meditative state and experience higher states of consciousness.

Meditation acts as a transition between my dream world in slumber and busy daily life. I approach my meditation with *kavannah*, which again in a form of feedback loop of consciousness, informs and deepens my meditation and reinforces my *kavannah*. Each morning, I am drawn instinctively to the special aura flooding my living room from the rising sun over the Biblical *Emek Refaim*, the Valley of the Ghosts. I sit silently, listening to the birdsong in the trees. This is preparation for quieting my mind. I try to empty mind from thoughts to sensations to stillness, to make contact with a sense of oneness. I enter into an eternal internal sacred space. Once quiet in body, thoughts and emotions, and accessing my breath, I detach myself to gain self-awareness beyond thought and concept. In this meditational state I am sometimes able to connect to a deeper consciousness allowing insights and revelations to emerge. Sometimes, I am able to glean information from my dreams, my artwork or by observing myself interact with others. As I go deeper, in touch with my spiritual direction, I connect to a place of serenity and introspection. I do not time my meditation, but let myself remain in this state of flow, usually 40 minutes. As I emerge, I often sense an expanded awareness or insight. I then focus on my conscious gratitude practice, by appreciating an act or event that happened in my life the day before. Gratitude is an essential spiritual attitude directed to the Divine with whom we have created personal communication.

Kavannah and Creativity

Early in my career, I developed a meditation practice as a prelude to engagement in creativity. I might read a verse from Torah or using a *niggun*, a wordless Jewish chant as I entered into my meditation. Today, I approach the process more intuitively and spontaneously, but meditation always precedes creativity. Jewish meditation and learning psycho-spiritual dimensions of Torah deepened the spiritual quality of my life and influenced my artistic process. My meditative practice transformed into a quest. Torah became a metaphor for a personal journey inward and outward, intentionally seeking a connection, a higher level of understanding, creating purpose in my life. As a calligrapher, the sacred Hebrew letters of liturgy and poetry danced in and among handmade paper collages. As a *Sumi-e* painter, I freely transformed images of the letters into abstracted flowing art forms. Ultimately, the concept of combining the arts with the letters and Jewish themes came out my synagogue experience with its music, meditation, chanting and dancing.

For many years now, I best express my deepest self through abstract expressionism, usually in shades of black and white. I am fortunate to be deeply influenced by a master Japanese artist and teacher, Yoshio Ikezaki. After first learning traditional Japanese handmade paper techniques, he surprisingly agreed to introduce me to *Sumi-e* painting, the technique of Japanese Ink Wash, which aims to depict the spirit, rather than the semblance of the painted object. Yoshio is a well-recognized master in the ageless Japanese tradition.

I am grateful for his mentoring and friendship for nearly thirty years.

Yoshio's Zen approach, starting with a meditation resonated with my own developing Jewish practice. He demonstrated and spoke to me of the concept of *Ki*, the life spirit moving the inks, as *Sumi-e* captures the essence of the object. "*Ki* is the essential element for my artwork. I use water as an active force to control the ink movement...*Ki* serves to transform my will and intention..." My affinity for the technique enchanted him. At the same time, he showed respect for my connection to Jewish tradition. As we explored ever more deeply the nuances of *Sumi-e*, he introduced me to abstract Japanese calligraphy yet encouraged me to express myself through the Hebrew letterform. Each letter, infused with its own mystical energy and meaning, became the perfect vehicle for my creations. As Rollo May describes, I experienced an "anxiously sharp sense of joy, a mild sense of ecstasy that came when I found the particular form for my creation." This fully expressed for me the essence of the Jewish spiritual artist within.

Synchronistic to working with Yoshio I was powerfully influenced by an exhibition at the LA County Museum of Art entitled "The Spiritual in Art – Abstract Painting 1890-1985". The goal of the exhibition was to demonstrate, as described by curator Maurice Tuchman, that "the genesis and development of abstract art were inextricably tied to spiritual ideas...to find new means to unite abstraction with mystical

"Images – *Tzadik*"

concepts, thereby creating meaningful images." In the wake of the exhibition I was able to put a definition to my own artistic direction, as a spiritual artist and an abstract expressionist.

In the studio, I feel a divine presence creating with me. My work is a focused awareness and an instant gesture coming from my soul. I experience a heightened sense of reality. I am in flow, so absorbed and totally involved in the experience that I create spontaneously and feel the power of the moment. I trust in the process as it moves within me transitioning through my brush into a painting with a life of its own. I entrust myself to the creative process in and of itself. I experiment, I play and enjoy the creativity for its own benefit. Outside the studio, in nature, where I experience the presence of the *Shechinah* most directly, I feel humbled and moved by the wondrous beauty and energy of all creation: spirits perceived in trees, oceans, sky and mountains, complemented and shaped by the force of winds, driving rains and crashing waves.

My spiritual home in Jerusalem, Kehilat Kol Haneshama, was inspiration for several art pieces which adorn the sanctuary. While chanting "*Kol Haneshama Tehallel Ya*, Let every breath praise God", the last line of Psalms at the end of the service, I experienced a visualization of the Hebrew letters. It inspired the design of the *Ner Tamid*, eternal light, engraved on fiber optic glass above the ark which later became our community's well-known logo.

Another one of my artworks *Halleluyah*, (reproduced here)

refers to the ultimate expression of praise and the end of Psalm 150, "Every breath praises God". *Halleluyah* hangs on a Japanese scroll, *kakemono*, at the entrance to the sanctuary. The design was carried out from a sketch my father, Ike, had done in response to my *Sumi-e* artwork integrating Hebrew letters, as in Japanese, vertically.

Torah and Spiritual Art

The Story of Creation in Genesis became a model for understanding the creative process. It all began with Divine creativity: "In the beginning God created, *bara*, the heaven and the earth" (Genesis 1:1). The verb *bara* is only used in reference to Divine activity and the supernatural ability to create something out of nothing. The beauty and awe that I experience in nature supports my belief that this wondrous creation can only be perceived as supernatural. "*Briah* is used in the Scriptures exclusively with reference to Divine activity, it refers to producing something out of nothing – *creatio ex nihilo*. There is no expression in Hebrew for producing something from nothing other than the word *bara*" (Rambam 1194-1270). The Vilna Gaon (1720-1797) explains that the word *bara* specifically designates "the origination of substance – a creative power that is beyond human power."

In human creativity, we create with a medium. The Hebrew word for art/craft is *amanut,* whose root produces words such as trust, faithful and amen, as said at the end of a prayer. Taken together, the Hebrew word offers hints to art's spiritual dimension. As an artist, *auman*, I have trust, *emuna*, in my creative potential and ability to stay faithful, *ne'eman*, to myself– all rooted in my faith in the Creator.

"And the earth was without form and void/chaos; and darkness was on the face of the deep" (Genesis 1:2). As an artist, I sense the concept of *tohu v'vohu*, void/chaos in Creation, as a metaphor for the beginning of creative expression. As I start my process, I encounter the void, even if just the blank paper, or the chaos, all the extraneous noise of daily life. It engenders a challenge. Here, I use both void and chaos as they relate to me, the individual, it may be anxiety, confusion or powerlessness, as well as the fear of having anything to say or merely the silent intimidation of an empty page or canvas. But "if you are to create, you must invite anxiety in," declares psychotherapist Dr. Eric Maisel. I need courage to delve into the darkness, the unexplored and unknown places of my psyche and into the depths, the essence of my being, to discover what needs to be expressed and give it form through my chosen medium. Through my explorations the possibilities reveal themselves. I must let go of the familiar to be able to create, I need to be in the unknown, the darkness and the depths, not knowing or planning what I am doing. These psychic situations are intimidating, yet transformative for change and growth, essential to a spiritual process of trust to achieve the "courage to create" that Dr. Rollo May refers to. Art requires emotion and integrity, producing something new that's uniquely mine.

By and by one learns to trust the process. Creativity emerges by exploring, experimenting, playing - delighting in the process itself. "And the spirit of God's vibrations was felt over the surface of the waters." I feel the blessings and vibrations that pervade my creative endeavors.

"God said 'Let there be light' and there was light. God saw that the light was good and separated between the light and the darkness. God called the light, Day, and the darkness He called, Night. And there was evening and there was morning, one day" (Genesis 1:5). Light and dark are the essential components of creativity. When we paint, for example, the contrast between these elements is at the core of the process. This is how we achieve expression: composition, highlighting, experimentation integration, and surprise in their interplay.

Spiritual creativity is the next step. "Let us make human

beings in our image, after our likeness. God created human beings in the divine image, creating them in the image of God, *b'tselem elohim*, creating them male and female..." (Genesis 1:26). I believe I am, you are, we all are creative human beings essential to God's process of Creation. Being fashioned in God's image, I also receive the gift of creativity. I am inspired by challenges to continue and participate in the process of Creation by being creative myself. Spiritual creativity actualizes itself when I invite God into my creative process and I feel ready to trust and let go. I feel the spirit of divine vibrations wash over me.

Meditation is an ideal space for letting go and developing trust. "And God formed the man of dust from the ground, and he blew into his nostrils the soul of life, *neshamat hayim*, and he became a human being, *nefesh hai* (Genesis 1:26-28 and 2:7) literally "a living soul". Hebrew uses two sets of words *neshama* and *ruach* to mean soul. Each also has another connotation—*neshima* (with only a slight variance in pronunciation) means breath and *ruach* means wind, the breath of the divine presence. Access to the soul is through the breath. Meditation is a transition between outside and inner worlds, where we seek to center ourselves in our souls. Breath is essential to meditation. I access spirit through the breath enabling flow when I engage in the creative process. In this serene place I contemplate my *kavannot*, my intentions, and find faith in myself to trust the creative process. I sense guidance to follow my intuition. Engaging in these pursuits of creativity and spirituality bring purpose and meaning to my life.

The divine-human partnership in creativity is highlighted in Exodus 35:30 and 36:1-3, with the choice of *Bezalel*, "in the shadow of God", to carry out the building and design of the Tabernacle, as well as the production of all the ritual objects. "Moses said to the children of Israel, See, God has proclaimed by name *Bezalel*...He filled him with Godly spirit, *ruach Elohim*, with wisdom, insight and knowledge, and with every craft, *melachah*... to perform every craft of design..."   Creation of the magnitude of *Bezalel* is the realization of covenantal relationship. In creating a physical sanctuary, a place to unite with God, "Creation is completed by its repetition as a human act; God's work finds fulfillment only as something of His power to create is imitated by humans," affirms Rabbi Arthur Green.

3

EXPRESSING THE KAVANNAH

"We meditate to find, to recover, to come back to something of ourselves we once dimly and unknowingly had and have lost without knowing what it was or where and when we lost it. We may call it access to more of our human potential or being closer to ourselves and to reality, or to more of our capacity for love and zest and enthusiasm."
Dr. Lawrence LeShan, psychotherapist pioneer in exploring therapeutic and ethical implications of meditation.

Meditation: Transition between Expressive and Kavannah

Meditation helps us transition between the outside and the private inner world; from the place of accepted behavior to the realm of intuition and knowing. Approaching each session without expectations keeps us open to growth by receiving new experience. Accessing the breath, quieting the body, thoughts and emotions, ideally, we detach from the noise of the day to gain self-awareness beyond thought and concept. In a meditational state we may connect to a deeper consciousness where insights and revelations emerge. At times, we may glean information from our dreams or apprehend our patterns of interaction with others.

Modern life is hectic. Everyone feels the pressure of deadlines, of being bombarded by electronic overload and constantly forced into multitasking. Perpetual stress puts us in a state of disstress. Meditation offers an option for finding silent space within ourselves and within daily life. But it requires discipline and commitment.

Paradoxically, the essential work is learning to do one thing at one time! Through cultivating a meditation practice, we may "comprehend a new way of perceiving and relating to the world...that brings strong serenity and inner peace."

On mundane and profound levels at the same time, meditation is the art of focus. Its practice creates relaxation, concentration and mindfulness. Focus, flow and introspection provide support and enhance the genesis of the creative processes. Through meditation, we access our inner being, tap into our innate creativity and discover meaning for ourselves. Meditation, *kavannah* and creativity have been very important vehicles to organize my life and give it meaning. Creativity and achieving the "Flow" state, first observed by Dr. Mihaly Csikszentmihalyi, is one of life's great gifts. "Flow is the state of optimal experience." Flow happens in moments of scientific discovery and insight, sports, nature, reading, creative projects or spiritual pursuits. Being in flow is enjoyable in and of itself, no matter the activity. Time passes without our noticing, as we wholeheartedly and fully engage in activities that give us pleasure and enhance our lives. Flow is focused, yet relaxed, work can be spontaneous or intensive planning and research. It can be accessed across the spectrum of lives' activities.

In Expressive Kavannah, we explore meaning through creativity. We strive to tap into our subconscious to express deeper experiences and images that support a reframing – a different perspective to view our world. In it, we transition through meditation into creative expression through flow. Meditation is the impetus for the creative, image-making, writing, music or dancing. From my own artwork and observation of my students' processes, I witness how the relaxed state of meditation connects to the flow experience. Expressive Kavannah emphasizes spontaneous image-making, without planning, thinking or judging. I am always surprised anew at how much all participants enjoy both the process and the product of expression from the depth of their psyches. They feel empowered. Living with *kavannah*, with intentionality, transforms even simple acts into opportunities for creating purpose. Daily relations with others, situations and tasks performed in light of *kavannah* allow us to actualize *tikkun olam*.

Jewish Meditation

Meditation has been part of my life since college when I was introduced to Transcendental Meditation (TM) popularized in the sixties by the Maharishi Mahesh Yogi. I continued to practice TM regularly until I was introduced to Jewish meditation. At the time I was living in Santa Monica. Synchronous with my learning with Yoshio Ikezaki, traditional Jewish meditation practices were revealed by Rabbi Ted Falcon at his synagogue Makom Ohr Shalom. My meditation practice changed dramatically. Forever! Meditation now flowed from the root of my being.

My practice of *hitbonenut* supports creative engagement. I experience both meditation and creativity seamlessly in flow, especially when the underlying *kavannah* is clear. The perceptions, insight and growth I am blessed to experience are part of my quest, contributing deeply to understanding myself as a Jewish spiritual artist.

Expressing the Kavannah and Creating Meaning

As both artist and teacher, I am open and intuitive. In an interview for a film on my exhibit **Images**, I shrugged with a wink and a smile, "it just comes through me!" I felt intuitively that the powerful experiences and therapeutic aspect of the art that was emerging in my creative process needed to be shared with others. Teaching technique no longer interested me. I wanted to reach people, move them and touch their souls. My quest broadened to encompass both artist and teacher with the express *kavannah* of healing mind, body and spirit of the other. Meaning in art, and not the incessant search for beauty and perfection, became paramount. I now felt a need to put these ideas into practice through facilitating of creativity and spontaneity.

With like-minded partners, artist Patty Flamm and actress Yvonne Hunter, we founded Studio Spiral, an art studio for children and youth. The three of us melded and merged our talents to develop a multi-media experience: a philosophy of encouraging imagination, self-expression and personal exploration through mixed-media art-making and drama classes. Every summer we created a new workshop with a country as the theme. For two weeks, the children were immersed in the culture of the chosen country through art activities, stories, drama, and music and even cooking! During the year, we offered classes separately and together, always engaging imagination and creativity, without regard to the final product. Working with the children was a total inspiration, as I observed their spontaneity, their imagination and their joy of creating!

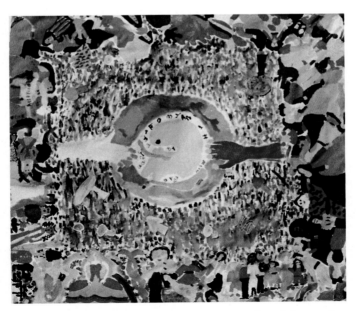

Studio Spiral youth and their group creation "Co-Existence"

"Art as Kavannah", the progenitor of Expressive Kavannah, is a process that I began to formulate and teach intuitively. It was based on my own discoveries and process as an artist integrated with insight of an educator. A sense of conviction about the spiritual in the art process and dedication to meaning led me to develop the teaching methodologies and concepts of Studio Spiral for adults. I already knew from personal experience that developing *kavannah* through meditation freed up artistic expression. I dedicated myself to freeing the artist within for adults, so they too could discover meaningful spiritual art. The goal was to enable them to experience the powerful act of creation that elevated the ordinary to the sacred using prayers, chanting, *niggunim*, wordless melodies, Jewish meditation and dreams. The flow created in these exercises carried through to the art making seamlessly. I had adapted my own spiritual artistic experience into a teaching format that worked. The Art as Kavannah concept comprised three components: a Jewish component, using meditation or introspective study; a hands-on self-expression or creativity component; and a processing or sharing component. The feedback was positive, and I continued to teach, research, experience, innovate, develop and refine the technique.

Gratefully, I was given the opportunity to experiment with the concept over two summers, 1995 and 1996, when I was Artist-in-Residence at the Brandeis-Bardin Institute in California. BCI, the Brandeis Collegiate Institute, is comprised each summer of two four-week summer sessions where college-age students from around the world are immersed in a total Jewish experience based on the arts, dance and drama, alongside intensive intellectual learning and even physical labor. Since that time, I continued to teach this method of self-expression and self-awareness at the Pardes Institute for Jewish Studies in Jerusalem and at my studio, Indigo.

Simultaneously, I was given a transformative gift. In <u>No More Second Hand Art: Awakening the Artist Within</u>, Dr. Peter London –

educator, art therapist and supremely talented spiritual artist – combined the spiritual with the therapeutic aspect of art. At the time I was focused on incorporating the Jewish spiritual tradition into teaching creativity. He describes this process "as a transformation from one-dimensional beings to multi-dimensional beings...the creative process employs a multi-dimensional mindfulness: intuition and reason, subconscious and conscious, emotion and intelligence, fantasy and memory and the spiritual with the material, mystery/unknowing with calculation, passion with the restraint of reason." Peter London, who I later befriended after a serendipitous encounter, made me realize that I was already doing art therapy intuitively. He expressed so clearly what I had sensed in describing myself as a transformative artist. Peter's therapy model inspired me to integrate his teaching into mine to create transformative experiences for my students. Understanding, embracing and teaching the concept of *kavannah* was to be its vehicle.

The development of the basic themes of Art as Kavannah was enriched by delving into the literature of Art Therapy. In addition to Peter London, Shaun McNiff's <u>Art as Medicine</u> was a critical influence. The more experience I gained, and the more I read, I became aware of a need for formal knowledge and training in the field. My friend and colleague at Studio Indigo, Tamar Einstein, herself a graduate of Lesley University in Boston, introduced me to The European Graduate School (EGS) in Switzerland. It was an exciting prospect to study with pioneers of the Expressive Art Therapy field to acquire the skills and knowledge necessary to effectively apply art therapy methods and techniques to a Jewish educational setting. EGS' emphasis is the dance, music, art and creative writing with therapy. This transfer, the shifting from one artform for to another becomes a new skill that serves the emotional process of clarification. I was stimulated and excited with this new model and sought to integrate it with Art as Kavannah. I found in the spiritual nature of Expressive Arts Therapy an important basis for the creation of Expressive Kavannah. Dean of EGS, Dr. Paolo Knill, writes "transpersonal considerations evolve from the traditions of the spiritual, religious and ritualistic use of the arts... Symbolic objects mark the place of worship...Great prayers traditionally are also great poems and do not lose their power through repetition...Music and especially song has the characteristic of calling or praising higher powers." I understood these concepts intuitively through my personal synagogue experience.

The Development of Expressive Kavannah

Expressive Arts Therapy provided an important learning experience for integrating the use of many art forms into Expressive Kavannah. The transition from one form of expression to another is one of the essential skills I became adept at teaching and facilitating to stimulate the imagination. Human imagination truly knows no bounds and is able to be expressed in numerous different manners and forms. I understood these concepts intuitively through my experiences of Jewish rituals: prayers, music, song and even dance used in praise of a higher realm. As they all flow together, I experience a state of oneness. Jewish identity and spirituality find inspiration in music, art, dance and poetry as they move us. The arts are crucial to Jewish culture and education adding a new dimension beyond the intellectual, the worldly and the tangible.

I personally felt the transformative healing power of art for the first time after my father's sudden death when I instinctively went for my brushes and ink. Dr. Shaun McNiff, my most influential teacher, later explained many concepts intellectually that I experienced intuitively: "the medicinal agent is the art itself". Providing a space for students to explore themselves through art making was a synergy between the physical use of the media and the creative process driving it, that engender healing and growth. Another of Shaun McNiff's messages, "trust the process" expressed the intuitive way I drew on faith and courage in approaching creative work. I felt empowered to use my own heuristic model to encourage and sensitize my students to the energy of their own creative process and rely on their inner wisdom. The expressive arts therapy model provided multiple opportunities to explore and integrate other art forms such as music, dance and creative writing with my art and teaching. Many new revelations in this experience were to come and I began to intuitively understand that "creativity is an ecology in which all the senses enrich each other."

Choosing McNiff as a role model in the Expressive Arts Therapy field seemed very appropriate both from a spiritual and professional point of view. There is always much more to learn from him. Shaun McNiff is authentic relaxed, open and easy to approach, as a man, teacher and facilitator. He spends a great deal of time getting to know each person in the class, memorizing their names. As he remembers each person's name, he puts them at ease. "Names are important". Explaining the work we would be doing together over the next few days, Shaun gently breaks down any awkwardness with simplicity, modesty and humor. As he taught me, "My job is to create a safe space, so you can make your egos become dust. I work very hard at that."

Getting to know the group sets the stage for the group work: contemplative art and healing. McNiff indeed provides a ritual space, a healing space. He speaks to the group about creating energies and an environment to allow a common purpose to heal one another together. A feeling of safety pervades the space. He encourages and invites trust, and planning what you are going to do as the only mistake. Let what needs to come, come through.

I had encountered the artistic concept of ritual space from Marc Chagall referring to his artwork as prayer. It influenced my grasp of kavannah, by sensing a common state of focus in my own prayer, meditation and artwork. Developing that space for my students presented a challenge aided by guidance from Shaun McNiff who equates healing and creativity. We need to take our problems, pains wounds and "do something with them", become engaged. He encourages students to share dreams as "dreams have a way of sharing what the reasoning mind can't get to. Try to stay with the dream, let it release its presence. Hold the dream and let it reveal itself and release imagination."

During the presentations and in response to the artwork, McNiff establishes a special atmosphere in accord with the intensity and seriousness with which he approaches the process. Firstly, he has all participants meditate on their work in silence and then respond and share with a partner, by the way a classic Jewish study method, *hevrutah*, with a great deal of sensitivity and intuition. In the presentations before the group, he focuses totally on the individual. His feedback for each student is positive and encouraging, at times he simply reacts to the beauty of the piece. He gently encourages each one to explore their relationship to images. Literally and figuratively, image comes from imagination, and as McNiff says, "imagination is the intelligence of morality." Imagination takes us into a deeper relationship with the world and integrates all the other realms.

McNiff further counsels: "First, sit with the image and meditate on it. Then, speak to the object as you, and let the object speak to you. As you personify the object, you start to get different voices. Speak as yourself first, the key is to see the object as a person. Then shift and let the piece speak to you. Get out of ego voice. The work is working with the imagination. It's a dialogue with the intelligence of the imagination that goes beyond ego thinking. It brings together all the other realms. It's the faculty of faculties."

Interestingly, medieval scholar Rabbi Moshe Ben Maimon (Maimonides 1135-1204) in <u>Guide for the Perplexed </u>(1185-1109) explains the role of the imagination for self-growth. "Part of the function of the imaginative faculty...is to retain sensory impressions, to combine them, and chiefly to form images. (However), the principal and highest function is performed when they are at rest in their action, for then it receives, to some extent, divine inspiration...this is the nature of dreams which prove true and also of prophecy."

Over the course of studies at EGS and subsequent classes in Israel, I experimented, watched, integrated and created in new modalities. Countless voice, movement, and poetry classes posed new challenges. Participating in music and performance arts, learning through experimentation and play, I learned how to absorb and respond to the energy of the group. From different ways to express feelings through the body I engaged in movement and dance therapy. I became more aware of body sensations in totally different and surprising ways. I learned from another teacher, Dr. Steven Levine that "the task of therapy is not to eliminate suffering, but to give a voice to it, to find a form in which it can be expressed. Expression is itself transformation; this is the message that art brings."

When we are faithful to ourselves, we can tap into our higher selves and express our truths. We cultivate *kavannah*, so we can focus on our spiritual essence. We seek self-actualization to expand our capacity to love and pursue meaning to achieve *eudaimonia*, altruistic living. "You think first of someone else" or "have a goal greater" than your immediate gratification, says Dr. Steven Cole, Director of the Center for Compassion and Altruism Research at UCLA. Each *mitzvah* we perform with *kavannah* leads to *tikkun olam*.

4

EXPRESSIVE KAVANNAH MODEL
GENERAL FRAMEWORK

Intentionally as Jews, we live according to the Jewish calendar. Weekly, we celebrate *Shabbat*, monthly *Rosh Chodesh*, and annually a series of holidays, some festive, some somber. On each *Shabbat* and major holidays we read a portion, *parshah*, from the Torah. These regular Torah portions provide an abundance of material for study and interpretation, especially stimulating for creativity the whole year long.

Expressive Kavannah integrates these cycles of holiday observance with models of arts therapy. The variety of arts expressions are readily adapted to the focus and mood of each holiday in a dynamic group process. While traditionally these practices take place within the family, in synagogue, or in *hevrutah,* a pair of study partners, Expressive Kavannah strives to create a context for experiencing and exploring the demarcations of sacred time in a personal, reflective and meaningful way. It becomes a vehicle for creating one's own *kavannah* as preparation for the communal event. In having read the Torah portion, for example, before you hear it read in synagogue, you can appreciate it in a different way that deepens the experience. In having prepared *kavannot* for *Yom Kippur* in the context of the class, the synagogue experience is totally personalized and unique.

My vision and *kavannah* is to support creativity, spirituality and growth. Creativity empowers. Spirituality deepens, and transformation enriches, heals and gives meaning to our lives. The creative process can be compared to a journey in four phases:

Home: Home physically and metaphorically is the most secure place I can be. It's comfortable and familiar. It is my sanctuary.

Leaving Home: As I first leave my safe space,I usually know where I am going and what I am doing but there is also uncertainty. As I walk down the street, I feel free taking in sights, sounds and smells.

Exploring my world: When I leave the familiar to explore my surroundings, I am open to the unexpected. This may cause me to experience unanticipated emotions: excitement, fear, frustration or fun and playfulness which require a spontaneous reaction.

Home again: When I arrive back home, I am different, something has changed in me. I am not necessarily readily aware of this. My experience and explorations have influenced and shaped me.

Megan – "The Journey Home"

This process is very individual. We each experience our own journey differently. The place of the void, *tohu v'vohu*, is where we learn to trust ourselves, an integral part of creativity, spirituality and transformation. McNiff's concept of "trust the process" states clearly: "If we are able to stay with a situation, it will carry us to a new place. The process knows where it needs to go...trust in the process assumes that there's a force that moves within a group, an individual or a situation that is distinctly 'other' and not subject to control." Leora remarked, "I ended the semester as a healthier and more vibrant person where creative expression and uncertainty play positive roles in my life."

Methodology of Expressive Kavannah

As discussed in the previous chapter, the model attracted me for its versatility and richness. When we use everyday communication, we often use a variety of different modalities to get our point across from speech, gesticulating, acting out, sketching and more, so why not in art expressions? Although primarily an artist, my training showed me the role of the imagination in providing a plethora of new expressions spawned by the initial inspiration. My students' transitions appear to happen with ease and produce surprising results. The order in which I present them here is a general model. As facilitator I don't participate in these activities, but I am there to hold the space.

Introduction – The introduction consists of four components: check-in, movement, journaling, Jewish learning.

Check-in – Especially with a new class, the introduction is time for me to meet the participants and for them to meet each other, as they will be working together for the next few hours. The intention is to facilitate connection. I like to have all participants say something about their name. Other times, I ask them to share something they want everyone to know about themselves. These brief stories create an interesting personal dynamic that helps every-one remember the names. Personalities are revealed very quickly: introverted, funny, spontaneous, or serious. In an ongoing group, the initial sharing may be deeper as trust develops over time.

Movement/Dance – Movement is the basis of awareness. We all need to express ourselves physically. Often what is happening in our consciousness is not available to us until we sense it in our bod-ies. So Expressive Kavannah starts with free movement, stretching or dance. Moving to music, feeling our bodies helps us let go. Always unstructured, usually accompanied by music and instruments, each in their own time is invited to move spontaneously. The body knows what it needs to do whether stretching, swaying, or dancing wildly to a release of inhibition and facilitates slowing down and focusing inward. Movement uses different senses, accesses another perspective and frees participants to work creatively.

Lindy dancing as Miriam

While free movement is an essential part of the introduction, it can also be elab-orated as part of a performance piece done in the image-making phase. In Song of the Sea, *Shirat Hayam* (Exodus: 15-20, *Be-shallach*), Miriam leads the women playing instruments in song and dance as part of the Exodus story. The class transitioned into spontaneous dance after studying and discussing the portion. "My favorite class was the one in which we each per-formed a response to Miriam's song/the song at the sea. Getting up and dancing felt wonderful," declared one student exuberantly after a sedentary day.

Journaling – Automatic or free writing lets participants be

spontaneous and intuitive. Most people come into a session preoccupied. The activity of journaling calms and focuses. It is totally personal. I try to encourage a daily practice, realizing full well that this might be the only time the person has given themselves this kind of time. Each journal is different, some for diary writing, poetry, drawing/sketching or a place to catch those good ideas before they fly away. Adam said, "whenever I sit down and actually start journaling, it just all spills out, and I realize how much I need it."

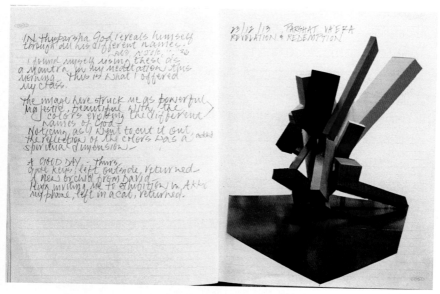

Edna – "Image Journal – *Va'era*"

<u>Jewish Learning</u> – My own Jewish learning and practice informs my teaching. I have been very fortunate to have been inspired by exceptional teachers. From the time I sensed my spirituality growing, I acknowledged the need to learn. I studied informally by choosing specific teachers, rabbis or scholars according to their particular specialty or took advantage of the learning environment I found myself in. I am blessed to live in Jerusalem, and in a lively center of progressive eclectic Jewish spiritual exploration.

The Jewish content of the lesson generally addresses the

weekly Torah portion, an upcoming holiday or a relevant part of the liturgy connected to those. I seek to connect participants to a part of the annual Jewish cycle. In the next chapter, I will elaborate on ways to select materials, verses, liturgy or foci within the holidays and later offer examples Expressive Kavannah classes utilizing those choices.

Creativity Period – The creativity component consists of meditation, image-making, creative writing, movement and music.

Jewish Meditation – The goal of Jewish meditation is to create in our lives a connection to God, for me personally to her feminine aspect, the *Shechinah*. Meditation is anessential component in Expressive Kavannah, accessing spirit through the breath, *neshima*, to usher in the creative process and support flow. My practice tends towards *Hitbonenut,* one of the types of Jewish meditation. It refers to the activity of going deeply into oneself to reflect and achieve understanding of oneself. As participants turn to focus on their inner world I guide them: "Find a comfortable position, and breathe deeply as I introduce the focus." Seed thoughts for our meditations in my teaching of Expressive Kavannah are distinctly Jewish taken from the Torah or liturgy and connect to our learning. An example might be the repetition of the word *shalom.* Even for those inexperienced in the practice, this aids students to turn inwards to access their creativity and transition from thinking mind to feeling mind. Usually I encourage a sitting meditation, with each person finding a quiet space until ready to move into creative expression. I believe the relaxation drawn from meditation induces a sense of flow which then continues into the image-making. In the image-making that follows silently, the meditative seed thought might continue to be chanted to enhance the atmosphere and support the "incubation during which ideas churn below the threshold of consciousness... incubation has often been thought the most creative part of the process," Csikszent-mihalyi suggests. "In meditation, I clearly saw an images and colors," says Rolinda.

Flow is a state of optimal experience, a state of mind in which we are totally absorbed and enjoy in and of itself. In Expressive Kavannah it supports spontaneous expression in the image-making. Without planning, thinking or judging, students enjoy both the process and the product which emerges from a deep experience. Meditation is the impetus for the creative aspect of the process, usually image-making, but also writing, and music making or dancing. Meditation offers an option for finding a silent space within, a pause from daily life to get to know ourselves again. By cultivating a practice of meditation, we create with quiet mind.

Image-Making – This meditative transition is the prelude and inspiration for image-making; silently holding a new *kavannah* born from Torah study and the connection to God. We are empowered to be creative as all of us were created in God's image. I observe the energy as students emerge from meditation totally inspired and motivated, choosing their media intuitively and spontaneously. From students' own accounts some see images in the meditation; others take in words of my teaching; while others follow their own newly created *kavannah* directly into the image-making experience. They "know" what they are doing facing the blank page, the clump of clay or a chosen object from nature. An hour is allotted to this part of the session as exploration and experimentation are essential for creative knowing. Images appear as students engage in their individual process with trust and enthusiasm. I join them working in my "Image Journal", but always remain available.

I intentionally call this creativity period "image-making", first for the therapeutic potential it carries. As Jung declares, "the image is a condensed expression of the psyche's situation as a whole." Secondly, for its expressive quality which is connected to imagination, as described by artist and art therapist Howard McConeghey: "An image...is like an angel, a messenger saying something, meaning something, moving us."

As participants emerge silently from meditation, they face a blank page. Yet, intuitively each one knows exactly what to do in continuing the flow created during the meditation. At first, I was surprised by the ease with which individuals choose materials sensually and spontaneously, awakening their esthetic responses by delving into the subconscious to externalize the images. Crucially, by design, students approach materials following the modalities of movement, meditation and study. I seek to facilitate a holistic experience of letting go and exploring meaning. It is important to supply media of high quality, varying from papers for collage, to paints, clay, pastels and found objects/materials depending on the venue. "We need somehow to find the correct fit between our purposes and the expressive power of each medium" states Dr. Peter London. I encourage experimentation with a variety of media which supports "knowing" through intuition and initiates the process of "art as medicine". At the end of a class at Hebrew Union College, Brett asked me where to buy pastels. "I am going to get a box of pastels and start drawing again. I should be grateful for the skills and faculties that I have." Liz declared how energized and positive she felt about herself and her life after the sessions.

As they engage, students learn to trust the process by permitting their internal landscape to emerge imaginatively in the unique and personal images they create. I enjoy my students' sense of mission to capture images or colors or feelings experienced in meditation or simply the intuitive knowing that they want to express. They are finding meaning coming directly from their psyches. Encouraging spontaneous exploration through the media, is healing in itself and also produces great motivation to find the "right" medium to express their own personal inspiration. They are involved in the same process as artists describe. Picasso declares, "Painting is stronger than I am. It makes me do what it wants." Jackson Pollack agrees: "The painting has a life of its own. I try to let it come through." Or according to Fernando Botero, "When you start a painting it is outside you. At the conclusion, it moves inside you. A piece is finished when it surprises and goes beyond original conception."

Creative Writing – Writing is an integral part of each Expressive Kavannah session, from the personal journaling we do at the outset to letter writing or poetry as a separate activity or even for some as image-making. Some are inspired by their images and spontaneously write on the backs of their works as a reminder of the process or the images used. Others write poetry in response to the image-making or as part of the flow. I also use letter writing as an exercise, such as letters to God as part of exploring Shabbat. As I learned from Rabbi Elie Spitz, a letter to God is a very effective therapeutic tool as we assume God knows us very well, so we are more willing to be very open and direct. Then, imagining a response from God provides insight and closure.

Poetry, again with emphasis on the process not the beauty of the expression, can be used after image-making. We look, examine and probe the image, writing associative words from it that form a poem. "I found the place inside where my own imagery emerges... a language of shape and movement, layers of color and light, echoed by journaling and poetry."Rolinda acknowledged that her poems inspired by images from Expressive Kavannah are totally different than without the process. Interestingly, her sister Tamara also expresses herself in the same spontaneous manner.

Movement/Music – In Expressive Kavannah music is used in many ways and for many different purposes as it supports the mood of each phase of the session. The music at the beginning of our session is to invite free movement or dance. I use both flowing and rhythmic music to encourage a variety of types of movements. Sometimes, instruments accompany our dancing. The choice of music creates a special atmosphere.

Occasionally, I use music or humming of a *niggun* for our meditation which may continue during the image-making. This tends to be quiet, soulful and meditative, to encourage an inward focus and fosters continuity into image-making.

Processing –

All of us desire our creations to be seen and validated and yet at the same time we are all sensitive to the feedback from others. Therefore, in my role as guide to processing, I have two major tasks. First, to "hold the space" and offer support in order to provide a safe space for the students who share their creations which express their deepest feelings and insights. Secondly, to create a dynamic among the other students to be "witness" to the process that is emerging by listening attentively without their associations or judgments. "Each session ended with a few minutes to write about our pieces before sharing them with one another. We viewed one another's creations, listened to what each artist had to say about her process. The shar-ings were precious, profound and deeply personal." The most valu-able way to support a colleague is to listen attentively to the person.

It is important to understand that value judgments can be positive or negative. Both "That's so pretty!" and "That's awful!" are value judgments. We must avoid both during processing. Each one wants to share their work, but we are usually ambivalent due to anticipated criticism or voices of judgment, which is why I constantly stress being non-judgmental. So, after experiencing many models of witnessing, my seminar group decided on the following model. Each person shares only if they want or only what they choose. Sharing is done individually with the group listening with free attention. Then, each one chooses whether to elicit feedback from others. McNiff again inspires us, "creativity is available to every person... this energy exists everywhere in life...we need others to fully realize our creative potential."

My training as an art therapist and educator served to hone

my sensitivity and intuition to be a better observer and listener. As facilitator I learned how to hold the space, fostering safety and trust. As I observe and listen to the processing, I sense who the person is and what they are expressing through the image. Gently, I probe, encouraging them to go deeper, to see, to connect and get a response from their work. Having experimented with a variety of artforms provided richness and surprises. Processing itself is intended to enhance the therapeutic process of creative expression, to gain perspective and resolve issues in our lives – a personal *tikkun*.

Creating the images is a period of self-discovery, while the processing period is one of consciousness-raising in a non-judgmental atmosphere of support and validation. Participants take time to witness their own work and spend time alone with it, looking, sensing, jotting down impressions. They are in dialogue with their image and talk to it as "You" rather than an "it". Approaching paintings as "ensouled" objects, echoes Martin Buber's I and Thou: "Spirit is not in the I, but between I and Thou... Man lives in spirit, if he is able to respond to his Thou. He is able to, if he enters into relationship with his whole being."

To set the appropriate tone for the processing phase, I developed a guide that I give each participant before we begin, "Engaging Kavannah and Midrash: Creative Interpretation". Jo Milgrom explains in Handmade Midrash: "The term *midrash* describes both a method and a genre of literature in which imaginative interpretation discovers biblical meanings that are continually contemporary". I was very fortunate to have Jo participate in my classes, we all learned a lot from her. Rabbi Arthur Waskow refers to making *midrash* as "the profoundly playful discovery of meaning between the lines of a (biblical) text", and he goes on to explain that "new forms of *midrash*-making seek to deepen our understanding of the world, ourselves and our relationship to our Judaism...it begins to seem possible for the *midrashic* process to put the *midrash* maker in touch with God."

ENGAGING KAVANNAH AND MIDRASH: CREATIVE INTERPRETATION

OBSERVATION: "I see purple"
See, look at the image you have created. Turn it in different directions.
Look at the negative space the image creates. Look at the colors you have used.
Look at it from a distance. Isolate elements that most speak to you.

IMAGINATION: "I imagine a path"
Do you sense a contextual meaning– PSHAT or an allegorical meaning – REMEZ? What colors, shapes, words catch your eye? Write words, associations you see in it.

REFLECTIVE LEVEL – DEEPER MEANING: "That reminds me of a time I went walking in the hills...."
Do you sense a metaphorical meaning – DRASH, or a hidden meaning – SOD?
Our images as our dreams, bring up deep meaning. These spontaneous creations come from our subconscious to get our attention. The processing can give us clues.

TIKKUN: Repair, healing are not usually apparent immediately but can create awareness and be the outcome of the integrative work done in the session and following it.

TEFILAH: What do you want to share with God?

In Expressive Kavannah we seek to draw inspiration from the biblical narrative, spontaneously and intuitively create an image to reflect a metaphor for deeper understanding of ourselves and our lives. Each detail we have chosen for this image is an "unknowing knowing" that is not available to us at the time as it resides deep in our psyche, our dreams, our meditations. "Through receiving and giving form to new images, we breathe new life into ancient scriptures and eternal teachings... (that) leads us to new places in ourselves" observes Pat Allen. As an artist who has always worked spontaneously, I understand I must wait for the meaning of my work. It may not happen right away but requires looking, sometimes in different directions, seeing, meditating, probing, getting glimpses of what I am expressing... but mostly waiting for it to emerge.

"When we look deeply at things; we get outside ourselves and become immersed in the object of contemplation. This meditation brings new and vital energy into our lives. This nonconscious way of being with the images is part of their healing qualities. We select things instinctively; and make them intuitively and live together with them in sensory relationships that exist outside the domain of rational thought" explains McNiff.

Different Types of Class Formats

Over the years, I have offered Expressive Kavannah in several frameworks: egalitarian Jewish Institutes, Rabbinic Seminaries, Progressive Jewish communities, as artist-in-residence in longer programs, retreats and private seminars. Each usually two-hour class is taught differently in each setting, emphasizing different foci according to the audience. I search for a variety of approaches to engage the spirit creatively for each in the group. Spirituality is engaged when we learn to trust the process, we are in. Creativity emerges by exploring, experimenting and delighting in the process itself.

In Rabbinic and Masters' programs, and college level institutes, Expressive Kavannah fits into the yearly curriculum. In these settings, the general focus is on intense, intellectual text study, and therefore introducing the arts is very challenging. My experience has shown students usingthe arts require a change of process from the daily intellectual, thinking mind to the creative engagement of the feeling mind.

Jewish learning is very cerebral and abstract, so producing a personal, concrete image supports both intellectual memory and meaning. Images created usually reflect individual interpretations filtered through personal history. Each person has a different perspective of what is meaningful. For example, when using text study of a Torah portion as a point of departure, I weave in creative experimentation, rather than student's day-to-day intellectual discussions. I encourage the association with the biblical narrative as a metaphor for a personal issue. "I really enjoyed processing this week's portion and connecting to it on an individual level," said Yaffa Shira. For example, when Expressive Kavannah studies the *Akeidah*, the Binding of Isaac, I ask students to personalize the concept of sacrifice in their lives. "What does the word sacrifice evoke for you? When did you make a sacrifice? How did it feel?" Going directly into meditation after this lesson, they are able to let go of the intellectual connotations and delve into their subconscious and emotive world.

Subsequent image-making allows them to produce a tangible visual for reflection which then can be processed in the supportive group setting. Text and images, intellectual and creative, complement each other and strengthen learning by enabling deeper reflection and integration. Pardes student Gershon remarked to me when I first started teaching there: "This class has provided for me a wonderful opportunity to process my learning in a very different way than I do the rest of the day. Normally, Jewish learning is very cerebral. In this class, by contrast, I am engaged in a visual and experiential process which has added depth to my experience."

Group creation: Jean, Adam, Jordana, Luisa and Lindy

In more eclectic Jewish institutes, such as Yakar in Jerusalem, I have taught a weekly two-hour class where I have the freedom to choose both content and structure. Although the content usually follows the weekly Torah portion or an upcoming holiday, the space provided, a large classroom, gives me the flexibility to emphasize different aspects of the arts, such as movement and drama. We can spread out, meditate in different parts of the room or work on the floor with no restrictions. This framework generates a very different feel than a formal classroom. The students are heterogeneous, of different ages, from different backgrounds and from varied Jewish streams. This makes for a dynamic, interactive teaching experience. "The open-endedness of the long sessions to explore creatively whatever was on my mind, and then process it in front of the group served as therapy for me during a tough year," remarked Abby.

Private seminars are more personal and ongoing, once a week for a year. The students get to know one another, some quite well, as many may have been working together with me over many years. Typically, a session will last two hours, and the structure is consistent with the general outline. However, I take the liberty to change the structure spontaneously or use different artforms to apply to different foci. Appreciating the processing and sharing with each other over a long period of time, these groups are mutually supportive and non-judgmental. The participants are embraced on their spiritual journey. The frequency of our weekly meetings establishes intimacy and trust, in turn allowing for personal and inter-personal growth. The more continuity, the more inter-connectedness, the deeper the experience. "It was a privilege to hear how the members of the group were wrestling with concerns of all kinds, and to watch how the work of their hands helped to heal their hearts," exclaimed Liz.

As artist-in-residence at the Brandeis-Bardin Collegiate Institute in California I taught in an intensive daily program over each of two one-month sessions. BCI brings together young adults to explore their Jewish identity through art, study and work. Here, I am part of an overall structured framework from morning until evening. I teach my arts-based class in the mornings, usually 3 hours, then participate in many of the other daily programs, which also includes intellectual study and prayer alongside dancing and singing. We are part of a community living in a magnificent outdoor setting, so nature provides important opportunities for inspiration and healing. "My experience with Expressive Kavannah was very spiritual and really helped me to find myself more and more," remarked Kelsi. The benefit of this model is its intensity. Meeting every day unifies the group very quickly, supports the integration of the technique and continuity builds creative impetus.

In progressive Jewish communities, such as Rabbi Elie Spitz's Congregation B'nai Israel in Tustin, California, I teach one-time workshops. This means that I don't have the continuity as in other frameworks and I don't usually know the participants. Therefore, I have to consider how to structure the technique so that the group integrates and benefits from the experience. For example, during my last teaching experience there, I focused on the *Shema* prayer, one everyone could relate to. This workshop is detailed in the chapter on prayers and blessings.

Retreats offer a very special way to experience Expressive Kavannah. We usually leave the city and our daily lives behind us for a few days to a quiet location in nature. In this setting I have collaborated with colleagues to provide unique experiences facilitated by specialists in their fields such as rabbis, dancers, writers or musicians. This type of workshop is enriching for both facilitators and participants, many of us in dual roles, as the collaboration fosters inspiration and creativity for all of us. The intensity of living together for a few days in a natural setting, this creative atmosphere is healing and mutually supportive and reinforcing. The experience of Passover in the Annual Holidays chapter is taken from a retreat in the Sinai Desert which had us crossing back into Israel mindfully, for its conclusion.

Lastly, I had a chance to teach my colleagues at the International Expressive Arts Therapy Association 2013 Conference. The context was not a Jewish one and the title of the conference was broad –"The Winds of Change". The title and abstract on my workshop were "Adapting to Change: Our Inner Voice". It read in part: "The Expressive Kavannah workshop integrates Expressive Arts Therapy with the concept of *kavannah*, focused intention, from *Kabbalah*. It is a spiritual model for Expressive Arts Therapy that offers participants the tools to gain self-awareness and perspective of their world. Self-awareness is crucial if we are to adapt to the changes around us. As the winds change, we change." Although I was given a very broad context, I was able to find a Jewish spiritual connection. In Hebrew the word wind is *ruach*, which has a double meaning, both wind and spirit. So, I used *ruach* as our focus for meditation which brought together our outside and inside landscapes. A uniquely beautiful experience arose out of the processing when a musician participant shared a moving *ruach* chant.

Last year, I was invited to teach my colleagues again, this time in New York at the Expressive Arts Summit. Unexpectedly, I was encouraged to present a Jewish topic on *Succot*, which was accepted. This was my first time doing Jewish in a larger forum, thirty people attended, some not Jewish! Collaborating with my colleague Sally Brucker, the session was called "Transformation at *Succot*". Our opening activity was creating a huge *succah*, hut, from rolls of colored crepe paper which the group really enjoyed.

Processing around collapsed *succah*

The Jewish holiday cycle provides the wisdom of a holistic model that stresses interconnectedness. In the Jewish tradition, *Succot* is a festival of great joy, based both on biblical and agricultural sources. Exploring its deeper meaning and personal associations reveals its potential for transformation. *Succot*, the joyous Harvest Festival in Jewish tradition, immediately follows *Yom Kippur*, the solemn Day of Atonement. This challenging transition happens in a matter of days. We explored how we adjust to that rapid change. This example of *Succot* is a metaphor to look at transformation in our lives. Participants practiced meditation to enhance flow and creativity; they experienced the transfer between art modalities, an important arts therapy skill to aid the focusing process; as well as how to personalize collective rituals to develop a unique and satisfying experience.

$$\boxed{5}$$

IMPLEMENTATION OF THE EXPRESSIVE KAVANNAH MODEL

"The person-centered approach…is …a way of being that finds its expression in attitudes and behaviors that create a growth-promoting climate…The individual has within himself or herself vast resources for self-understanding, for altering his or her self-concept, attitudes and self-directed behavior – and that these resources can be tapped if only a definable climate of facilitative psychological attitudes can be provided."
Dr. Carl Rogers

Expressive Kavannah is a contemplative personal process facilitating our life's spiritual journey, to awaken creativity and deepen Jewish identity. It combines Expressive Arts Therapy with the wisdom of Torah and *Kabbalah*, the Jewish mystical tradition. The model is process-oriented, as opposed to our daily product-oriented lives. Offered in an inviting atmosphere of learning, Expressive Kavannah is focused creative exploration and spontaneous self-expression. You, or your participants, are invited to be open to the creative process and enable the imagination to do its magic. Using Jewish meditation, combined with a variety of artforms (writing, movement, singing, music, image-making) Expressive Kavannah is a profound educational experience that supports personal growth and self-awareness. Envision that you are facilitating a spiritual connection and empowering others through the arts by offering an opportunity to synthesize and give voice to participants own individual process of discovering new meaning in their lives.

The Role of Facilitator

The facilitator of Expressive Kavannah may be a teacher, a rabbi, a therapist or even an artist or other lay person. Of utmost importance is to cultivate a non-judgmental attitude and approach in order to set the tone for using the arts to facilitate other's self-expression. You need courage to commit to going through your own personal process of introspection to develop your personal *kavannah* to assist and guide others in developing theirs.

Facilitating Creativity – As the facilitator, your goal is to stimulate and inspire. In addition, facilitating Expressive Kavannah, requires you to cultivate and clarify your own mindset, how you perceive the world, and *kavannah*, your intention, through introspection and awareness to empower spontaneous deep and meaningful expression for others. We project who we are when we facilitate. Your authenticity inspires trust and openness. You are a whole person with other interests, hobbies and talents. Strive to integrate these to enrich the experience. By integrating topics and ideas that excite you, a special energy is transmitted: being open to new ideas, seeing the familiar in new ways, observing your surroundings and noticing details for inspiration. These are sometimes to be found in the most unexpected places. Every day we are exposed to interesting stimuli but we are not necessarily aware of how to apply them to our personal or professional lives. (Refer back to the creative journey in chapter 2. Home, Leaving Home, Exploring the World, and Back Home). Every day we confront change as we are exposed to new experiences, even on the most mundane level. We are in contact with others from whom we learn. And, hopefully, we also stop, quiet ourselves to receive and become aware of those experiences and their effect on us. Of critical importance is demonstrating a true interest in and acceptance of each student, and a non-judgmental and positive attitude.

Creativity, making something out of our imagination, requires openness and courage to try new ideas. It is about learning and un-learning, trial and error and freeing oneself to explore endless possibilities and potentialities. The process evolves and changes as we learn to trust it and ourselves. "The process knows where it needs to go" is an important message for participants who are afraid to make mistakes and do not yet trust themselves. Trust builds in a supportive atmosphere of exploration as part of the learning process.

Teaching Jewish Content – Teaching a Torah portion or a holiday with *kavannah* is about your personal life: your relationship to Jewish practice, beliefs and values, connection to God and ultimately how intentionality expresses itself in your life. This entails a personal spiritual and philosophical introspective pursuit. Consider first how your own spiritual pursuit can be integrated into your facilitating. The complement to this introspective process is intellectual inquiry. Make it come alive! Connect the biblical narrative or holiday rituals to real-life situations and problems. Personalize them. For example, with the *Akeidah,* the Binding of Isaac, and the concept of sacrifice, ask yourself "How do I experience sacrifice?" Think of all the innovative ways you might engage others in experiencing sacrifice in their lives. In one workshop we split into pairs and bound each other's hands to replicate the feeling. Ask your students how they experience sacrifice in their lives. Present experiences that will help each person access what is meaningful for them. The goal is to build an authentic personal ritual to prepare for the holiday and celebrate it in a way is purposeful for them.

Designing the Workshop – First, coordinate with the institution and venue. This is both technical, organizing details about scheduling, timing and space, as well as substantive, understanding how Expressive Kavannah fits in with your student's overall educational framework.

Next, know your group. The make-up of the group guides your decisions about both content and forms of artistic expression. If you want to focus on a Torah portion, be clear what you want for your group. For instance, in one particular group the students had studied the Torah portion in *hevrutah* twice during that week. The process of Expressive Kavannah "helped me see the big picture," said Becky. As a result, I took a more general approach by asking "what stood out for you in the portion?" Once you've chosen the text to focus on, designing the experience flows: text to texture!

Move on to selecting a meditation related to the text, as well as supportive music and movement. Imagine for yourself how you might want to make images. From there it is easier to select appropriate materials for your students.

Implementation – Implementation requires the facilitator to be teacher and holder of the space. First, you are responsible for setting up the space, giving directions as to how the program will be carried out, and managing the timing of the various components. As teacher you present the Jewish content and guide the discussion. Whether you have simply selected one verse from a Torah portion or a general theme that relates to a holiday, the way you offer it becomes the basis of your student's explorations.

Being holder of the space mainly relates to the facilitation and processing aspects of the whole experience. This is critical especially when the participants are sharing their process and work. You are, and ask the others to be, attentive, empathic listeners, as well as making sure each one is given equal time. Each person sharing must feel that you particularly, and the others as well, have the utmost respect for their individual process and work.

The Role of the Group

Crucially, Expressive Kavannah is a group activity. While the initial sharing may appear to be a social activity, it readily becomes a support group as participants share their creations and intimate feelings relating to them. Participants experience creativity as a positive personally beneficial outlet. They feel validated by the empathetic listening of the others. There are a few aspects of the group which are important to understand. The group also has to be apprised of certain rules for the better functioning of the experience. First, from the time the meditation ends, the transition to the media and image-making take place in silence. They have experienced deep introspection and it is important to stay inside themselves. The processing also requires attentive listening and a show of respect and support for the person sharing. One last comment is to try to take a few minutes at the end to get feedback from your participants. This is important for you and for future experiences.

Daylong Expressive Kavannah retreat

Expressive Kavannah can be facilitated with any size group. The size of the group determines how personal and intimate the experience will be, particularly in the processing part which can be intimidating in itself. My preference is a maximum of twenty, even though I have successfully worked with larger groups. So, if you have the option of limiting the number of participants that is the best solution. The major parts of the program, writing, movement, learning, meditating and image-making all can be facilitated in a large group. It is the processing that changes in larger groups, so I ask them to choose a partner to share with one-on-one, like *hevrutah.* Each person takes turns quietly listening to the other for an equal amount of time. When the whole group reassembles, you can then ask that each small group share one important aspect of their experience.

Physical Requirements

Space –The optimal space for a class or workshop is one with tables, but also includes an open area for movement or dance. On the other hand, at the Brandeis-Bardin Institute where I had 75 people, we used a big hall and the participants did their image-making on the floor. If the indoor area is not large enough for free movement, then try to find easily accessible outdoor space. Being outside can be very inspiring and participants seem to easily find their own spaces.

Media (Materials)–The basics:

- A computer, CD or instrument(s) for music to accompany the class during writing, movement, meditation and image-making. Choose the music to create an appropriate, supportive atmosphere.
- Image-making materials: paper, pens, markers, glue, construction paper, magazines, clay, etc. The more and greater variety the better, but Expressive Kavannah can also be facilitated with very simple office supplies.
- Important note: I never refer to the image-making as "Art" with a capital "A", although the art therapy field does. Non-artists may be intimidated by the term. Expressive Kavannah is about making images that are meaningful for each

individual, not for show or exhibition. Use of various visual arts media facilitates producing images without preparation or planning. We seek spontaneous, subconscious creation that draws upon deeper information unlocked from our psyches during meditation. It is process and not product, without value judgments about skill, quality or beauty. Creating images is for individual self-expression and the attendant benefits for well-being. Creating "Art" raises fears of judgment and inadequacy. Each one of us, created in the image of God is inherently creative, only requiring a bit of support and encouragement to experiment.

Expressive Kavannah Model in Action

Following is a brief example of the flow of an Expressive Kavannah class or workshop:

Introduction – With students who meet on regular basis I have each of them share a personal event from the past week. With a one-time group, or a new group, I ask each one to share their names and something they would like everyone to know about them.

Movement – I put on music and ask them to freely move or dance to the music. If there is adequate space, you may ask them to do so with their eyes closed.

If there are instruments, I encourage them to use them too. If you play an instrument (I unfortunately do not) that is an added benefit. If someone asks what they are supposed to do, I gently respond that their bodies will tell them what to do. It's all about letting go, relaxing, being in the moment.

Writing – If students keep journals fine, if not provide paper. You can suggest a topic such as gratitude or forgiveness that may or may not be related to the teaching or simply ask them to "journal" or engage in automatic writing. Writing is meant as another support tool to facilitate letting go. Writing is private and confidential, not for sharing.

All three of these first elements may or may not be related to the general theme. They can be regular exercises which are used in each class to provide a consistent framework. Alternatively, you can tie them to the main focus you have chosen for the workshop or class.

Jewish Teaching/Framework – According to the choice you have made as a focus for the class or workshop, this can vary from a verse taken from the weekly Torah portion, a coming holiday, or a prayer. This element is described extensively elsewhere and following this part there is an example from *Lech Lecha* (Genesis 12:1 - 17:27).

Meditation – I typically allow students to sit in meditation for ten minutes, but you can determine what is appropriate for your group. This is the most direct spiritual component. It is the place of quiet, connection and inspiration which also promotes relaxation. A relaxed class or group is a true gift. As Judaism is infused with God Talk, this is the opportunity to choose a verse from the Torah which express a divine-human communication. Let participants experience and explore the concept for themselves in silence.

How to facilitate meditation: Ask participants if they have experience with meditation as this will give you a sense of your audience. If most of them have little or no background, I recommend putting on quiet meditative music, perhaps a chant or *niggun* and have them sit quietly, eyes shut and allow the music to take them where it will. If they have some experience, you can offer a "seed thought" meditation using a Jewish mantra such as *"Sha - Lom"*, repetition of the *Shema*, or a word from the text or blessing.

Image-Making – Participants move directly from meditation, at their own pace and time, to the media table to choose their elements and tools. A typical question in painting is how to achieve a certain colorsince I only provide the primary colors (red, blue, yellow) with black and white. If you are asked a technical question you are not sure of, tell them to try it and explore. The only way for them to really learn is to find out for themselves and then they will remember for the next time. You the facilitator are there for support, encouragement, technical questions and to time the activity.

Processing – This final stage in every class or workshop is anticipated positively as a period of self-discovery and consciousness-raising in a non-judgmental atmosphere of support and validation. Because of its importance, I would like to expand here on the processing component for the benefit of facilitators who desire to offer their students an optimal therapeutic and educational experience.

We are all sensitive to feedback from others, yet at the same time we want our creative expressions to be seen and validated. We are so used to being criticized and defending ourselves. "The voice of judgment is instilled in childhood, when our parents, teachers and other authority figures tell us how to behave...This is internalized, and we carry it with us for the rest of our lives," commented a student, Margaret. She added that I "set the scene, so we can work with no fear of the judgments of others", validating my having facilitated a safe environment of trust to work in.

"Meditation on the significance of the image for its maker... furthers the making of the art. Meditations on images and talking about them amplify their expression and help us to see things we did not see before," says McNiff. Therefore, the processing in Expressive Kavannah has three stages to it: alone, together with the facilitator and finally with the whole group.

In Expressive Kavannah the facilitator must remain neutral yet supportive. You can use words like powerful, colorful, interesting, strong, or evocative linking them to examples in the work itself. Then try to probe the process. Participants may not be satisfied with the work, but it still important to have a sense of what it was they are trying to communicate. Please ask them not to discard work there and then, but to give it a chance to 'speak' to them over a few days.

All of us desire our work to be beautiful, yet it does not always come that way. Many of us have difficult messages from the subconscious that we have tried to deal with in our images. As facilitator, it is truly wonderful to see and appreciate each individual's creativity and variety of expression. Try to express that wonder and appreciation as you assist each participant in processing their images.

- **Alone** – Each participant is asked to sit quietly and meditate on their images. The intention is to deepen the sense of *kavannah* in the image, how it feels to them, what does it mean for them.

- **With the facilitator** – My training served to hone my sensitivity and intuition, to be a better observer and listener. As facilitator I learned how to "hold the space," which is an arts therapy term for "the physical presence of someone trustworthy (who) allows the seeker to relax conscious control" in order to explore their own personal process. At this stage, the facilitator is the only one permitted to offer feedback.

  After the individual meditation and processing the image, the goal is to deepen perception and draw out the feelings about the experience. I ask each participant to share and listen attentively to others to support the creative process that is emerging. I give personal and individual feedback to encourage each participant in their joint creative and spiritual quest. Facilitating with sensitivity means letting the participant talk, giving each one space to integrate, to make individual connections and gain insight and awareness. This activity must be carefully timed so as to give each person time to talk equally.

- **With the Group** –My students sometimes opt for having their colleagues give their feedback to get a different perspective on their own image. Similar to the facilitator, this must be done with sensitivity and without value judgments (neither positive nor negative). I oversee this component, which is directed to both individual and group processes. In most cases, in my role as guide to this process, I work hard to create a dynamic among the students by setting up norms and boundaries. Others in the group offer their insights on the images and creations with respect and sensitivity. Participants share their work, only if they choose, both material and emotional, meaning they share the product and their processes of spirituality, inspiration and deeper insight. "Staying with the image demonstrates how the object before us is an opening to the soul," encourages McNiff.

- **The Product -**If any participant does not want to share the product that's fine. However, it is important to at least try to draw them out to talk about their images. Usually it's because they lack the self-confidence and have judged it negatively for themselves. This is hardest type of judgment to break through. In our society we are product-oriented and judgmental. We also strive for beauty – our ultimate value. When we visit a museum, go to a performance, a play, or a concert, we are quick to judge without sufficient background knowledge of the artist's work, her intention, process, or choice of expression.

Follow-up and Feedback -Feedback from students is critical for the teacher, but it may be equally important for the student. It is a way for participants to express themselves personally about what 'works' for them and what doesn't. Find ways to brainstorm, share insights and develop ideas together. Expressive Kavannah is about sharing creativity and spirituality and learning from one another.

The following quotes show feedback from various students

about their experiences of Expressive Kavannah. I also share how their insights have benefitted me in relation to my own intentions and efforts. I am grateful to all of them.

Luisa: "This class has opened up new entrances to my understanding and emphasis when I pray and study from Jewish sources." The combining of all of the arts approach is powerful in that it influences on many different levels. Yaffa Shira: "Expressive Kavannah served as a forum for seeing the big picture. Each week it was an opportunity to reflect on connections between the texts. I looked forward to this release to look at things from a different perspective. The class gave me a more expanded approach to the text and I regularly take out the pieces I made in class to ponder new approaches." Both these students similarly described "the big picture" or "a different perspective" that enabled them to comprehend their intensive text study. We need many different viewpoints to learn, absorb and integrate knowledge and information as our own. In Art Therapy we call this "reframing". It apparently is a very important to the holistic process of *tikkun*.

Hayim: "Expressive Kavannah was very important... it allowed me to process both my learning and my emotional development...in way that would otherwise have been lacking." Another, Lindy: "This class allowed me to integrate some of my other learning in a non-intellectual environment and also allowed me a spiritual and creative outlet that otherwise would have gone by the wayside." We are multifaceted human beings who need to be functioning on many levels concurrently. Working with creativity and spirituality brings up and clarifies emotion and enlivens.

The atmosphere of open, mutual creativity using a contemplative model, the processing and validation component appears over and over to provide a meaningful experience for each person's needs. Abby: "The open-endedness of the long sessions to explore creatively whatever was on my mind, and then process it in front of the group served as therapy for me during a tough year." Liz: "It was a privilege to hear how the members of the group were wrestling with concerns of all kinds, and to watch how the work of their hands helped to heal their hearts." Both these students benefitted from the therapeutic dimension of Expressive Kavannah. Having work witnessed and being able to process it are healing activities.

Liz: "I was always energized and amazed about how positive I felt about myself and my life after the sessions." And Leah: "I ended the semester as a healthier and more vibrant person where creative expression and uncertainty play positive roles in my life." These two students drew on the magic of "art as medicine". The creative activity, the support of the group, and the validation of their work contributed enormous "positivity" to their beings and their lives.

Brett: "Expressive Kavannah has been the single most productive, positive and inspiring program that I have ever participated in and run myself. When I first participated in the program, something cracked loose in the greatest way. Because of this program I have discovered a passion for painting that I will continue for the rest of my life. More importantly, I have run this program several times with 5th and 6th graders. In one iteration, each student was given their Hebrew name and its English translation as their prompt. The responses were wonderful, but one response still stands out in my mind. She said, 'I didn't know that my Hebrew name could be a part of who I am.' To make the connection between oneself as one walks into the program and between the person one discovers oneself to be, is the miracle of this program."

Creating flow in our lives is an optimal state of being. It is described by Dr. Mihaly Csikszentmihalyi: "Flow involves living fully, completely involved in the present moment, a focused awareness, enjoyment, and creative experience that is rewarding and of itself". This is what we are striving for – a total experience.

$$\boxed{6}$$

PRAYERS AND BLESSINGS

"Prayer clarifies our hope and intentions. It helps us discover our true aspirations, the pangs we ignore, and the longings we forget. It is an act of self-purification, a quarantine for the soul. It gives us the opportunity to be honest, to say what we believe, and stand for what we say. For the accord of assertion and conviction, of thought and conscience, is the basis of prayer…Prayer is the essence of spiritual living."
Abraham Joshua Heschel

Prayers and blessings are the building blocks of each ritual observance. Expressive Kavannah gives us a way to approach the familiar from a completely novel perspective, unlocking new meaning and revelation for ourselves.

The Hebrew word for prayer is *tefilah,* from the Hebrew root, *pellel,* meaning to think, entreat, judge, or intercede. Its reflexive form *l'hitpalel* means to pray or to judge oneself. Jewish prayer, when approached with *kavannah* and with a strong emphasis on blessings and benedictions, becomes a time of introspection and self-evaluation.

Historically, Jewish prayer was transmitted orally by a leader, the *shaliach tsibur,* or public emissary, which led to a host of personal variations and improvisations. These idiosyncrasies became known as *kavannot,* the plural form of *kavannah,* as the crucial attribute was "participation of the heart" as opposed to the retention of the mind. One example of biblical prayer, Moses entreating God to heal his sister Miriam, is a spontaneous and direct cry for help to which God responds by healing her.

Prayer provides an opening. The most important part of any Jewish prayer is the humility and introspection it provides in our developing a relationship with God. In it we learn to love God and to know we are loved. We learn to listen, to argue, to obey, to disobey, to be forgiven. In the process we learn to pray. *Kavannah* brings respect, sincerity and introspection to prayer, enabling us to focus on knowing and understanding what we are praying about and think about its meaning. The liturgical melodies provide an additional support for this process of focus.

The advent of the *Chazal*, an acronym for "Our Sages, may their memory be blessed" changed the nature of prayer. They formalized the liturgy (Greek: public works) by designating rules as to prayer time (*shararit, minchah, maariv*) with a fixed order and structure to the prayers, which were compiled in the prayer book *(siddur – seder – order)* governed by Jewish law, *Halachah.* Jewish law is the collective body of religious laws derived from three sources: the written and oral Torah; laws instituted by the rabbis; and longstanding customs. Many of these prayers and customs have become tradition and have lived on until today.

Observant Jews are constantly reminded of God's presence. Upon arising is a prayer thanking God for returning our souls as well as prayers for enjoying any material pleasure; prayers to recite before performing any *mitzvah*; prayers to recite whenever some good or bad thing happens; and prayers to recite before going to bed at night. All of these are in addition to formal prayer services three times a day every weekday and additional times on *Shabbat* and festivals as required by *Halachah.*

With the advent of Jewish renewal and an ensuing age of spirituality, the heterodox Jewish lifestyle is more popular today than ever, particularly in the U.S. It creatively integrates many different traditions and practices. "Jewish wisdom knows no denominational boundaries, after all, the Torah was given to all Jews at Mount Sinai, not just those identified with one movement rather than another," declares Rabbi Lawrence A. Hoffman. Integrating the spiritual into our daily lives gives us a new perspective of focus. We no longer are the center of the world, God is. "The Jewish dictum is 'Know the God of your father,' because self-knowledge is meaningless outside of the greater context. One can only know oneself by referring to the whole of existence and seeking one's role in it, the seat of one's unique-ness, as given by the Creator," says Dr. Yair Caspi. We are indeed challenged to create a personal Jewish practice to support this spiri-tual journey. Exploration and introspection guide us to discover which traditions and rituals will enrich our lives and give it meaning. It is the mindset of *kavannah* that engenders the humility to appreciate the Creator for our bounty and the openness to receive the ultimate connection.

The Shema: Judaism's Fundamental Prayer

In Expressive Kavannah I usually teach prayer in the context of *Shabbat* or holidays. The major exception is the *Shema* which is an excellent choice for teaching a new, unfamiliar group since most if not all Jewish participants are familiar with it. After all, the *Shema* prayer is the essence of Judaism. It expresses the idea that God is one and that we accept Him fully as our higher entity.

"Hear, O Israel, The Lord our God, the Lord is One.
Blessed be His Name, whose glorious kingdom is forever and ever.
You shall love the Lord your God with all your heart and with all your
soul and with all your might. And these words that I command you
today shall be on your heart. You shall teach them diligently to your
children and shall talk of them when you sit in your house, and when
you walk by the way, and when you lie down, and when you rise. You
shall bind them as a sign on your hand, and they shall be as frontlets

between your eyes. You shall write them on the doorposts of your house and on your gates." (Deuteronomy 6:4-9)

First, we accept oneness and then we are commanded to fully and completely love Him. With our love of God comes responsibility (response - ability). We are asked to observe and fulfill the commandments that He bequeathed us. These basic principles of morality must always be with us in our consciousness, on our bodies with *tefillin*, phylacteries, and on our houses with the *mezuzah*, a parchment encased and affixed to the doorpost of Jewish homes.

In their everyday lives, observant Jews follow the commandment to recite the *Shema* twice a day, upon waking and going to sleep. In the traditional prayer service, we recite the *Shema* immediately after taking out the Torah. Before its recitation we are asked to fully concentrate on fulfilling the positive commandment of loving our God, by enunciating each word clearly. "*Shema* requires *kavannah*. This *mitzvah* which affirms God's unity presupposes thoughtfulness, so must be accompanied by *kavannat halev*, heartfelt intentionality," declares Rabbi Daniel Landes. To reinforce the *kavannah*, we cover our eyes with our right hand and recite each word carefully out loud emphasizing the final letter of the final word, "*echaD*", the Hebrew meaning "One". The last letter of the first word, *ayin*, together with the last letter of the last word, *dalet*, spell the word "*ed*", which means witness. We say the *Shema* out loud as a declaration confirming its acceptance.

Teaching the *Shema* is a fundamental lesson in monotheism. God is One/Oneness. I choose it for the Expressive Kavannah work as the *kavannah* it requires is equally important as the words pronounced. Exploring oneness can be a spiritual mind-body experience as each needs to sense or feel what this means for them. Even though not done in every repetition of the *Shema* in synagogue, I suggest having participants declare the *Shema* out loud while standing, inserting their own names instead of Israel thus making it more personal by speaking out loud directly to the essence of their being. This emphasizes personal responsibility. Both the verbal and the physical reinforce our commitment.

The *Shema* prayer can also be used as a meditation – inhaling and exhaling each word. Or participants can meditate on the mystical concept of "oneness". Focus on feeling the oneness in body and soul, *neshama*, aids envisioning one's own connection to the Divine. Or consider what the concept "God is in the details" might mean to you. The variety in the image-making highlights the uniqueness of our creativity and expression, in relation to our personal experience of the universality of *Shema* – how it touches each of us and the medium chosen to shape it.

Sharon and Mindy –"The *Shema*: We are all one"

As an artist, I particularly love the *Shema* because it is the prayer written on parchment contained inside the *mezuzah.* The outer casing has no specific requirements except for the letter *Shin,* or the full word, *Shaddai (shin-dalet-yod)*, another biblical word for God who we are calling upon to "protect the doors of Israel". Thus, the shape, form, color, and even material are all left to artistic inspiration. The meditation and ensuing image-making can be coupled with *mezuzah*-making. Having led workshops over the years, I have facilitated many creative *mezuzot* being made. The most memorable and enjoyable was part of a Sinai Passover retreat. I joined the group in *mezuzah*-making from objects found in nature and we wrote our own prayers.

Blessings – Building Blocks of Prayer

Every blessing is at its core a prayer since it either expresses gratitude to God or asks God to help accomplish what we cannot do on our own: confession, petition, or praise. It invokes divine-human participation and co-creation. The words *baruch* and *bracha* are both derived from the Hebrew root meaning "knee" and refer to the practice of showing respect by bending the knee and bowing during certain blessings. Every time we say *baruch* we are showing humility. "To bless is a radical act," says Rabbi Ted Falcon, as every blessing is an opportunity to bring the sacred into our lives and connect directly with the Creator. Blessings are easy to identify as they usually start with the word "*baruch*" and continue with the phrase "*Ata Adonai, Eloheinu Melech Ha-olam* —Blessed are you, Eternal One Our God, Universal Being". "... '*Baruch Ata*' engenders humility. '*Adonai Eloheinu*' relates to the two aspects of God: '*Elohim*' the God of acceptance, and '*Adonai*' the God of transformation," affirms Rabbi Harold Schulweis. When we say a *bracha*, we are expressing our gratitude and our awe of God. There are traditional blessings for almost every occasion, which gives us the opportunity to spontaneously touch the sacred. "If you are looking for the heart and soul and bones of Hebrew prayer, you will find them all in the blessing. A *bracha* is a special kind of utterance that can turn a moment into an event. Blessings intensify life by increasing our awareness of the present even while awakening our connections to the past. In a richly faceted world, full of surprise and infinite variation, the source of blessing is everywhere to be found," offers poet Marcia Falk.

Blessings in Expressive Kavannah

Similar to prayer, teaching blessings is usually incorporated into teaching of *Shabbat*, holidays or as part of the learning about the Torah portion from which they are taken. For instance, in *Parshsat Naso* (Numbers 6:24-27), we find one of the most important blessings in the Torah, known as "The Priestly Blessing". In the early days of the First Temple the priests were ordered by God to bless the community at the Holy Temple every day.

"May God bless you and safeguard you.
May God illuminate his countenance for you and be gracious to you.
May God lift his countenance on you and grant you peace.
Let them place My Name upon the Children of Israel, and I shall
bless them."

This last verse explains that it is not the priests who bless the people. Rather, it is through them that God blesses the people. From an ancient *midrash*: "Though I ordered the priests to bless you, I will stand together with them and bless you."

From the time that Abraham was blessed by God and given the power to bless, the blessing became the privilege of those elders with divine connection to channel their energy upon others – a truly divine-human collaboration. The patriarch acts as a link between generations. The blessing that Jacob gives to his grandsons Menashe and Ephraim in *Parshat Vayechi* (Genesis 48:20) is a paradigm of the same blessing and understood as a blessing for Joseph too. Joseph's ability to maintain his spiritual integrity in exile was that his sons were now worthy of this status: "May God make you like Ephraim and Menashe". We need God's protection so as to be enlightened to move beyond the physical to the spiritual. We need to understand our purpose and understand the greatness of God, our Creator. Peace is balance in our lives: holy/mundane, soul/body, inward/outward.

The book of Genesis in the Torah emphasizes blessings and there is also an abundance of blessings in the prayer books for almost any occasion. The use of the Priestly Blessing today varies with the practices of the different communities. In Orthodox circles it is uttered only by *"cohanim"* in accordance with their priestly status. They cover themselves with the *talit* prayer shawl and spread their fingers in the form of the Hebrew letter *shin,*"ש". Generally it is found in the *Amidah* prayer, as well as being used at the conclusion of special rituals and for individuals. As a general practice it is used to bless children by parents as part of the *Erev Shabbat,* Sabbath night, rituals.

"Priestly Blessing"

I have chosen the priestly blessing as an example of a divine-personal connection to use for our Expressive Kavannah work. The spiritual and creative inspiration it provides for the arts has been touched on many times. We are creative as God has blessed us with this potential. Another reason for the choice of the Priestly Blessing is its long-lasting importance in Jewish tradition. It is cherished still as part of the orthodox service by *cohanim*, descendants of the priests, and on *Shabbat* evening to bless our children. Precisely for this reason, it has an endearing quality which we often hold special memories of either being blessed by our parents or of blessing our children.

Since this blessing has always been a joyous part of my family's *Shabbat* evening celebration, allowing my husband and I express our ongoing gratitude for our children being part of our lives, I really enjoy teaching it as part of Expressive Kavannah. I not only relate to the aspects of the blessing cited above, I also try to integrate its precepts into the meditation portion of the class. For meditation, I'd like to suggest using the imagery of the narrative's scene of the Priests at the Temple blessing the Jewish people or simply repeating the word *"shalom"*, being granted peace, to generate personal memories of blessings, the role of blessings in your life, how to bring in the spiritual. The images that emerge from the psyche may support in retrieving long lost situations which in turn can inspire visual images, dance, poetry or music to explore new meanings for yourselves.

7

JEWISH HOLIDAYS

Jewish life is governed by the ancient lunisolar calendar of our ancestors. It determines the timing of the weekly observance of the Sabbath, *Shabbat*, and the annual observance of festivals, such as *Rosh Hashana*, *Yom Kippur*, *Succot* or *Pessach*. *Shabbat* and holy days are differentiated by adding special prayers and blessings. Rituals vary according to holiday, each with their own mood, from blasts of the *shofar* on *Rosh Hashanah* to the introspection of *Yom Kippur*, building and dwelling in huts on *Succot*, to the reading of the *Haggadah* at *Pessach*.

Expressive Kavannah utilizes the daily, weekly and annual observances as a framework for transmitting Jewish learning content to develop student's intentionality in approaching each observance in turn.

Shabbat: The Sanctification of Time

Shabbat is equally essential to Judaism as the quintessential *Shema* prayer. There are few ideas in the world of thought which contain more spiritual power than *Shabbat*. Our tradition claims that on that day we gain a *neshama yetira*, an additional soul (Exodus 31:17). Heschel declares: "The seventh day is like a palace in time with a kingdom for all."

The period from twilight on Friday until the appearance of three stars on Saturday evening, is known as *Shabbat*, the Sabbath day. It has its own feeling and mood as its "primary awareness is one of our being within the Sabbath." Friday evening services, *Kabbalat*

Shabbat, welcoming or receiving the Sabbath, celebrates the theme of creation. *Shabbat* is a remembrance of God's act of creation, followed by rest. "On Friday evening as our family begins *Shabbat*, I sometimes imagine God, having created the world in one very packed week, finally taking a break. 'God rested and was refreshed' (*Shavat va-yinnafash*). This mythical image enables me to pause, slow down and appreciate Creation. By observing *Shabbat*, I am imitating the divine," says Daniel Matt.

The imagery for *Kabbalat Shabbat* is invested with a distinctly feminine feeling, as both Creation of the physical world as well as the *Shechinah* are imbued with feminine energy. The mystics viewed Friday night as a wedding between Israel and the *Shechinah*. "*Lecha Dodi* – Come my Beloved", chanted early in the Friday evening service suggests imagery of both Queen and Bride. The *Shabbat* morning service, by contrast, changes to a masculine energy with a serene and intellectual mood as the Torah is read in synagogue. The Torah reading and *drashah*, sermon, are the central part of the service. Both before and after the reading, the prayer leader parades the Torah scroll through the sanctuary, so each congregant can touch and kiss it. *Shabbat* ends with the appearance of three stars in the sky and another brief differentiation service, *Havdalah*, drawing the distinction between holy and profane, between the Sabbath and the other days of the week. A new week begins with the greeting "Shavua Tov", have a good week.

Abraham Joshua Heschel refers to *Shabbat* "...which we build anew each week. It is made of soul, joy and reticence. As a weekly discipline its atmosphere is a reminder of adjacency to eternity. Indeed, the splendor of the day is expressed in terms of abstentions, just as the mystery of God..." For many, those restrictions do not appear relevant to our modern lifestyles. As with blessings and prayers in the preceding chapter, I would like to encourage the heterodox, liberal Jews to create a contemporary spiritual *Shabbat* practice that is meaningful to them.

My colleague Rabbi Elie Spitz's spiritual approach encourages us to "create space for *Shabbat* as it is vital for renewal and growth." Jewish practice offers us the gift of *Shabbat* as a "day off" from the stress and demands of our fast-paced technological contemporary world. We all need a day of rest and relaxation once a week, a time to tend to ourselves, body and soul. So, to fully enter into *Shabbat* to heal ourselves only we, each of us, can create a practice that supports our health and lifestyle. Spitz describes *Shabbat* as "a bridge between the Divine and our social lives, integrating the various dimensions of our inner and outer lives."

I live in Jerusalem, so my experience of *Shabbat*, our day of rest, has a timeless and peaceful quality. As the city shuts down, *menuchah*, I affirm creation by not engaging in work, *melachah*. On Shabbat I rest from what I do the other six days of the week. As a liberal Jew I let the everyday physical world slow down and get revitalized by a meaningful practice that I created. Nothing is more important or holier than *Shabbat*. It takes precedence over every other ritual or holiday.

It is important to me to transmit its sanctity and facilitate an Expressive Kavannah experience for participants "to enter into *Shabbat*" through their learning and meditation. Therefore, preparing for it with the appropriate intention is crucial. Each separate act, starting with lighting the candles to receive its embrace, to welcoming the *Shabbat* bride in prayer and in song, to reading the Torah portion, offers precious teaching material for Expressive Kavannah.

In Expressive Kavannah we take time to listen, learn and explore the concept of *Shabbat*. In our journaling we might consider how we enter into it? How would we like to enter it? What makes it meaningful for us? This is not an intellectual decision. It comes from our heart and soul to feel what touches us, what resonates for us and do we need to change anything to make it "right" for us?

For meditation the rich imagery of the *Shabbat* bride provides a singular visualization to stimulate imagination. *Shabbat*, the day of rest, was itself the creation of the seventh day. In the words of the *midrash:* "This is comparable to a king who prepared a wedding chamber but was missing a bride. Similarly, the world was missing *Shabbat*" (Bereshit Rabba 10:9). In addition, the traditional *Kabbalat Shabbat* melody, "*Lecha Dodi* – Come my Beloved", is a joyous melody for the meditation.

Rolinda – "*Shabbat*"

Annual Holidays

The Hebrew calendar is "lunisolar", both lunar and solar. Following the cycle of the moon, the beginning of each Hebrew month, Rosh Chodesh, is marked by the new moon and all major holidays occur on the full moon. However, years are calculated according to the sun, so "leap months" are added to synchronize moon months with annual solar cycles. Similarly, we are simultaneously touched by both lunar and solar cycles in our spiritual lives. The Jewish festival cycle is inspired by the natural world and its seasons, historical events and myth. Certain holidays relate to agricultural harvests, such as Shavuot and Succot; others recall major historical events, such as the Exodus from Egypt; some combine both.

The annual cycle of festivals has a profound effect on the human connection to season and time. Jewish holidays imbue all seasons of the year with spirituality. By mindfully observing and celebrating them we grow our relationship with the *Shechinah* and the world around us. "Simultaneously, a second spiritual cycle, the weekly cycle of Torah readings, also start and end during the High Holiday season from one year to the next on *Simchat Torah*. If the sacred calendar traces the path of the soul, then the Torah is the path of that heart," professes Rabbi Alan Lew.

Starting with *Rosh Hashanah*, literally the head of the year, our calendar takes us on a spiritual journey through the year: re-connection and renewal at *Rosh Hashanah* with the sound of the *shofar;* the solemnity and awe of *Yom Kippur* characterized by de-votion and abstinence; the joy of *Succot* in building and decorating the *succa;* the craziness of *Purim;* rebirth and freedom at *Pessach,* Passover; and the anticipation of revelation at *Shavuot.*

The festival cycle in Jewish life provides a collective context for a full range of emotions, customs and rituals. Expressive Kavan-nah provides a supportive and healing framework to prepare for each holiday in turn through personal reflection and expression. Celebra-tions, as individuals and in community, are more impactful when we approach them with the kind of focused, directed intention, the *kavannah* that we are able to develop in our group work.

High Holidays

Critically important to the High Holidays – *Rosh Hashanah* and *Yom Kippur* – is the concept of *teshuvah,* traditionally translated as response, return or repentance. *Teshuvah* is a journey, a process taking us through events and actions of the past to guide us cur-rently in life. It can also mean turning, a fork in the road, a choice of personal direction and commitment, particularly as it relates to our connection and annual re-connection with the Divine.

Rolinda – "*Masa Acher*, a Different Journey: Collage for the New Year"

Preparations start a month earlier at the beginning of the Hebrew month of *Elul*. At the core of traditional observance are the forgiveness prayers, *selichot*, that prepare us for the upcoming holidays. It is a month to engage in a soul accounting, *hesbon nefesh*, through prayer, introspection, and meditation to look deeply into ourselves and our interactions with people, place and the divine.

Again traditionally, the High Holidays are a matter of life and death; on *Rosh Hashanah* we ask to be written in the Book of Life for the coming year; and on *Yom Kippur* we seek for the decree to be sealed. *Yom Kippur*, also known as the Day of Judgment, is the culmination of this period. A 25-hour fast enhances our detachment from the material world; we fill the day with penitential and confessional prayers and await the final verdict. As twilight deepens, the final blast of the *shofar,* the ram's horn trumpet, signals the end of the fast. We are filled with anticipation of the joyful celebration of the *Succot* festival that comes a mere three days later by building a *succah* to celebrate being forgiven for our sins and a successful Fall harvest.

Rosh Hashanah

Rosh Hashanah celebrates Creation, *Yom Harat Haolam.* It is a time of renewal and rebirth, a celebration of life itself. We seek to renew our days as of old, *hadesh yemenu k'kedem,* or as I teach in Expressive Kavannah to "make the old new." A time to examine ourselves and our relationships, a time for giving charity and a time to reconnect with our spiritual roots.

Our *selichot,* forgiveness prayers of *Elul,* set the tone for *Rosh Hashana.* In the Torah, it is referred to as *Yom Hazikaron,* the Day of Remembrance, as we are reminded to take on "three trans-formations...remaking our lives, refreshing charity, and reconnecting with our spiritual roots," says Rabbi Waskow. It is also called *Yom Teruah* – the Day of Trumpeting – sounding the *shofar,* which is a primary symbol of *Rosh Hashana.* We fulfill the commandment of hearing the sound of the *shofar,* truly hearing its resonance deep within to awaken the process of review and the possibility of repen-tance and renewal. Its soulful piercing sound calls us to transforma-tion, expressing what can't be said in words, blasting our prayers into the gates of heaven. Hear the metaphor in its blasts: *tekiah – she-varim - teruah,* whole – broken – whole.

In selecting teachings for *Rosh Hashanah,* you might focus on the theme of trumpeting, blowing the *shofar* (it is always nice if someone in the group is able to properly blow the *shofar,* I confess that I cannot), or the theme of remembering the creation of the world. I have often selected chants from the *Rosh Hashanah* service, such as the powerfully complementary *Avinu Malkenu* and *Shechinah Makor Hayainu*. *Avinu Malkenu* is a prayer which supports us in our task of renewal. Translated as "Our Father, Our King," it is a metaphor written by *Chazal*, our sages of blessed memory, for the positive relationship people need to strive for with one another. If all of us are subjects of the King, it was posited, then we owe each other the respect of an equal. At *Rosh Hashana*, in deeply and honestly facing ourselves, striving for renewal and repair, we seek a feeling that a transcendent being cares about us. In addressing God directly, the *Avinu Malkenu* lends itself to an intimate connection with God, an important theme in this book. Standing with the ark open, we prepare ourselves to receive. Following I have chosen a few verses from the prayer which emphasize our personal relationship and therefore the requests we might make.

> *"Hear our voices- Listen to us, respond to us.*
> *Hear our prayers- Accept our prayers.*
> *Recognize our imperfections – See our desire to*
> *improve, notice our efforts.*
> *Inscribe us in the Book of Good Life – This is our*
> *prayer for a good life.*
> *Fill our hands with your blessings - Bless us, sup-*
> *port our spiritual journey.*
> *Renew us with a new year – We want renewal, we*
> *are ready to change"*

As a complement to the *Avinu Malkenu*, I often teach another well-known prayer *Shechinah Makor Hayainu* – Shechinah, our Source of Life. Together these chants bring into the Expressive Kavannah circle both masculine and feminine energy to accompany us on our *Rosh Hashana* journey.

> *"Remember we are your sons and daughters*
> *We strive to feel a close relationship.*

Teach us to walk with grace
Help us find a positive path in our lives.
Teach us compassion and righteousness
Help us learn to be upstanding and moral.
Turn our suffering to joy and grief to delight
May we feel your presence in hard times."

My intention in teaching these chants is to help students in opening themselves to enhance the spiritual experience at *Rosh Ha-shanah*.

Another approach that has worked well is to start *Rosh Ha-shana* Expressive Kavannah sessions by asking students to review their year in writing, initiating a *heshbon nefesh*, accounting of the soul. Ample time should be allotted for this process which ideally may continue throughout the High Holidays. You may follow this with sharing, if there is willingness, or teaching more deeply about the importance of facing oneself courageously in the mirror of our soul. This takes the place of journaling which in regular classes or work-shops is often the first activity. While journaling is also an opportunity for reflection, a soul accounting is more demanding and challenging. As a facilitator I adopt a neutral stance with a clear intention to en-courage introspection, reflection and a willingness to change or allow for the possibility of transformation. Rabbi Alan Morinis elucidates the process: "The central point of *heshbon nefesh* is to reveal to con-sciousness the contents of the unconscious mind. These are, by defi-nition, hidden from us. But because the contents of our unconscious are perfectly reflected in the patterns of our deeds, certain images return night after night, and the patterns become unmistakable. We need this truth about ourselves to guide our steps on the path to deep, lasting, fulfilling transformation."

Following the writing and sharing or teaching, you may choose to initiate the meditation with either the *Avinu Malkenu* or *Shechinah Makor Hayainu* chants; first singing in unison, then as a *niggun* silently, then carrying the niggun inside. I still marvel at how participants emerge from meditation, moving silently, with their own developing *kavannah* into creative image-making for processing and understanding of the holiday and how it touches them.

Finally, another theme to use for *Rosh Hashanah* might be the *shofar* itself. Typically, in biblical times the *shofar* was the Jew's way to announce events – the onset of *Shabbat* and holidays, to announce victory, to communicate from mountaintop to mountaintop messages from afar, and so forth. Today it is blown throughout the month of *Elul* as a reminder that the Days of Awe are upon us. *Rosh Hashanah* is also called *Yom Hazikaron*, the Day of Remembrance, with the sound of the *shofar* reminding us that this is the day we reconnect with God, who remembers us in our *teshuvah* process.

Definitely if you choose *shofar* as a theme, it is important to have a *shofar* to share. I would not recommend that you have participants try to blow *shofar* as you will find that the discordant sounds are distracting. However, if you or one of the participants is capable of blowing the *shofar*, then by all means incorporate the actual calling of the blasts or play a recording. At times I also use the sound of the *shofar* as a support for meditation. Hearing and feeling its blasts and vibrations deep within us arouses many deep connections. It is a powerful instrument and medium which has provided inspiration for many creativity sessions.

Yom Kippur

Yom Kippur, the Day of Atonement, is celebrated ten days after *Rosh Hashanah*. The intervening days are called the Days of Awe. At *Rosh Hashanah*, we turn to God, to help us transform ourselves, to recognize limitations and patterns, aspects of strength and of weakness, to find the strength and wisdom to better ourselves. At *Yom Kippur* the atmosphere is solemn, the world is suspended in judgment, in preparation for the final reckoning. On this day, we devote ourselves totally, body and soul, to the *teshuvah*, repentance, and *vidui*, confessional, processes. We fast for 25 hours to reinforce our spiritual commitment to lead from thought to action.

In reviewing the past year, in examining ourselves, trying to see without illusion who we are, first we must engage in self-forgiveness, our hardest task. Then, we strive to "love thy neighbor as thyself." We live in community, not in isolation. Forgiveness must be sought and or offered in relation to the other people in our lives. We can pray to God to forgive us, but we must face ourselves and encounter the other in order to engage in real forgiveness.

As the holiest day of the Jewish calendar, *Yom Kippur* offers a wealth of themes to structure an Expressive Kavannah class around. You may choose to focus on the many powerful contemplative prayers, on the baffling and provocative Book of Jonah, or the giving or offering of forgiveness.

Traditional prayers on *Yom Kippur* seek forgiveness collectively and communally. Together in synagogues around the world, we gather to chant *Kol Nidre*, "All our Vows" declaring all invalid, null and void. *Yom Kippur* eve is known by the name of the magnificently haunting *Kol Nidre* melody. Starting that evening we publicly accept a long list of transgressions, *Ashamnu, Bagadnu,* etc. The entire congregation stands, each beating one's chest to internalize their personal participation in the collective's transgressions, recited as a confessional, *vidui,* and in so doing seek to be inscribed in the Book of Life.

Another aspect of forgiveness I have taught relates to the ethics of forgiveness, particularly from whom, how and when you must seek forgiveness. My understanding of this matter was borne of a personal experience. Every *Yom Kippur* I tried to let go of my pain and forgive the two people who had caused me so much anguish in my life. No matter the intention, no matter the effort of imagination, I was never successful. I just couldn't do it. It wasn't until I attended a lecture and teaching offered by Rabbi Joseph Telushkin at Kol Haneshama, my home community, that I finally made a break-through. First of all, he teaches that you are not obliged to forgive unless the other has sought you out. If you seek out another to offer forgiveness and the other fails to reciprocate after two attempts, you are no longer under any obligation to them. Most importantly for me, neither are you obliged to forgive people who have done you irrepa-rable harm. This was a revelation for me. I felt liberated. I encourage everyone to seek the guidance of Rabbi Telushkin's <u>Code of Ethics</u>.

In teaching Expressive Kavannah on *Yom Kippur*, I often refer to the Day of Atonement as the Day of At-one-ment, a word-play concept in English developed in the Jewish Renewal movement sim-ilar to what is often done in Hebrew. As one engages in the process of *teshuvah* in relation to our actions and omissions, and seek the crucial forgiveness of others, we seek to achieve wholeness. This inner process strives to bring us to a state of repair, of connection that will lighten our load and facilitate action. Ultimately the inten-tion, or *kavannah*, is for participants to deeply consider their personal *vidui* processes, enabling a return to a sense of integration. I ask: "What is your own personal and private confession, your words, your meaning, your *kavannah*? What are your issues, who do you need to forgive and from whom you must seek forgiveness? Expressive Kavannah is about making meaning, creating *kavannah* for yourself. You can shape your own ritual, as well as your own healing.

Another approach to the work on *Yom Kippur* is focus on the communal prayer of confession. The traditional *Ashamnu* is an alphabetic acrostic, consisting of 24 lines recited in the first-person plural. I have participants read the prayer, and then the complemen-tary *Vidui Mashlim* in the first-person singular. Next, I encourage them to create their own confessions in their own words. The idea of moving from the communal to the individual is to encourage personal reflection and responsibility for our own actions. Students have later shared that they found that this created a more impactful experience during the holiday.

Following is the English translation of *Ashamnu:*

"We have trespassed, we have dealt treacherously, we have robbed, we have spoken slander, we have acted perversely, we have wrought wickedness, we have been presumptuous, we have done violence, we have framed lies, we have counselled evil, and we have spoken falsely; we have scoffed, we have revolted, we have provoked, we have rebelled, we have committed iniquity, and we have transgressed; we have oppressed, we have been stiff-necked, we have done wickedly, we have corrupted, we have committed abomination, we have gone astray and we have led others astray."

Just as there is great value in confessing our limitations there is also great value in acknowledging our strengths to continue our work of *tikkun olam*. To stimulate positive energy I have also utilized a "Positive Vidui" by Rabbi Avi Weiss:

"We have loved, we have blessed, we have grown, we have spoken positively. We have raised up, we have shown compassion, we have acted enthusiastically, we have been empathetic, we have cultivated truth. We have given good advice, we have respected, we have learned, we have forgiven, we have comforted, we have been creative, we have stirred, we have been spiritual activists, we have been just, we have longed for Israel. We have been merciful, we have given full effort, we have supported, we have contributed, we have repaired."

I strive for a total process which lets participants engage in forgiveness, feel the heaviness lift and then feel good about themselves with the above positive assertions. This is **at-one-ment**.

Jean – "The Rock"

"The kavannah for Yom Kippur was forgiving someone. I decided I wanted that someone to be God. I had a friend who was dying of cancer and the pain of it is physically a rock in my chest during the meditation. I drew a dark, heavy, round rock glinting with graphite. Around it appeared the satiny contours of a shell…the rock appeared to be floating above it. As time passed it occurred to me that I want to do another drawing…wherein the rock becomes a pearl." Jean

There are abundant choices for seed thoughts for meditation (refer also to those used for *Rosh Hashanah*). I enjoy using two in particular. First, a walking meditation to the music of Ernst Bloch's Cello Suite for *Kol Nidre*, to simulate the somber mood of the service and engender an attitude of humility. Walking reinforces the mind-body aspect of this meditation and the concept of encountering the other. Second, I lead a sitting meditation of personal forgiveness to facilitate the inner process. I ask them to visualize, one by one, those who may have hurt them, or that they may have hurt, whether intentionally or by omission. From this deep space they transition into the image-making: "At *Rosh Hashanah* it is written, at *Yom Kippur* it is sealed."

Succot

Succot, the festival of booths, is considered by some to be an integral part of the High Holidays. It marks a sharp transition from the stern, judgmental atmosphere of *Yom Kippur*, to the joyous harvest festival. *Succot* instills a new sense of trust in God's providence of abundance, fulfillment and hope after being forgiven for our sins. A wonderful transformation happens in this short period of three days. The *succah*, the booth we will occupy for seven days, is itself a new home to decorate and fill with one's own spirit.

The *Succot* festival derives from three biblical sources. First mentioned in Exodus (34:22), it is agricultural in nature, the "feast of ingathering at the year's end" celebrating abundance in the Land of Israel. A more elaborate religious significance is found in the commandment from the weekly portion of *Terumah* (Exodus 25:8): "Let them build a sanctuary that I might dwell among them." It is complemented by a later commandment in *Emor* (Leviticus 23: 24, 39, 42): "You shall live in huts seven days...in order that future generations may know...I brought them out of the land of Egypt. I am the Lord, your God."

I share with students my own rapid transition from introspection and forgiveness to joy and celebration. I use the Expressive Kavannah process to provide an opportunity to reflect our own swings in mood, emotion and spirit. I encourage personal expressions related to the harvest and its metaphors: how we till, sow, and reap to support inner associations in today's urban environment. The theme of God living among us in the sanctuary we have built for Him, touches on our spirituality and ritual in our lives. The Exodus from Egypt relates to our concept of freedom, its significance and how it actualizes in our lives. Lastly, living in huts for seven days, we give up our well-appointed homes to remind us of the temporal sense of life, a return to simplicity and our values of spirituality versus materialism.

You may find a different approach to teaching *Succot* by emphasizing the biblical sources and traditional customs. According to *midrash*, this period marks the building of God's sanctuary, the *mishkan*, tabernacle, in the desert. It is a time of gathering the building materials for the *mishkan,* as well as the much simpler *succot,* the booths themselves. The basic mitzvot (commandments or good deeds) of *Succot* according to the Torah are: to build a *succah* and live in it, and to gather the four species – *etrog* citron, *lulav* palm fronds, *hadas* myrtle, *aravah* willow. *Emor* 23:40 reads: "You shall take the product of goodly trees and rejoice before the Lord" for ritual use in the service.

In addition, you may also consider a focus on other themes, such as: the symbols of your *succa;* the meaning of the four species for you; the metaphor of wandering and coming home, hospitality and guests. Often during a meal in the *succa* we ask one another who we would like to invite into our *succa* as *ushpizin*, special guests. Traditionally biblical figures, but equally effective with any historical figures or loved ones who have passed on, having everyone imagine their own guests allows each one to personalize the experience.

I usually select the *niggun* of *Succat Shalom* from the weekly *Shabbat* service. I guide a visualization of who you are and your relationship to the *Shechinah.* As this is a holiday associated with beauty and the *mitzvah* of *hiddur succah*, beautifying the *succa*, it inspires us to ponder our personal concepts of beauty. Start with chanting together and then following the *niggun* internally. I have also guided meditations related to "What do you want to plant, sow or harvest?" After which, you can ask participants to create a poem from their theme. As incongruent as it may sound at first, I often suggest the form of a Haiku: three lines with a 5-7-5 syllable structure. I ask them to describe the subject with sensory detail, with concrete images and descriptions, in the present tense and end with a surprising last line.

"I visualized a place for G-d to be with me. I imagined myself sitting on the rock, shaded by the flowering succah, listening to the chuckling and whispering of the stream, surrounded by grass, wildflowers and sun.

During Chol HaMoed, I went camping with friends. This project walked with me, and reminded me, as I slept in nature, by mountains, seas, oceans and streams, that I was by G-d."   Miriam – "*Succot*"

Chanukah

Several months pass by before we have our next holiday, *Chanukah*, the Festival of Lights, which is celebrated at the juncture of the Hebrew months of *Kislev* and *Tevet*. This corresponds roughly to the winter solstice as the days grow shorter and the nights longer. We experience the extremes of light and dark. As in many other traditions, myths and folk practices the theme is to bring light into the gathering darkness around us. It is one and the same miracle of illumination celebrated by lighting the *Chanukah* candles for eight days.

A famous *midrash* illustrates this situation: When Adam saw the days getting gradually shorter, he said: "Woe is me, perhaps because I have sinned, the world around me is being darkened and returning to its state of chaos and confusion; this then is the kind of death to which I have been sentenced from Heaven." So, he began keeping an eight-day fast. But as he observed the winter solstice and noted the days getting increasingly longer, he said: "This is the world's course," and set forth to keep an eight-day festival (*Avodah Zarah* 8a).

The word *Chanukah* means rededication, as in *chanukat*

bayit, popularly known as a "house warming party". *Chanukah* has a few essential themes that you may use in the teaching part of Expressive Kavannah. Some are inspired by historical events of the Maccabees' battle with the Greeks, a miracle of faith achieving an improbable victory; freedom from religious persecution; or the miracle of the holy oil lasting eight days. We sense Divine presence in those events, alongside the element of awe and the deep faith it took to even dare light the Temple *menorah* marking a time of re-dedication and renewal. As we light the *menorah* in our own homes, we imagine the light as a flame in our souls that will burn on through our lives.

Aliza – *"Chanukah"*

I usually choose a classic Jewish meditation on a candle. We consider the dynamic ever-changing movement and separation and integration of the colors of the flame. It never looks the same, but its core remains unchanged. It gives of itself to light the others but remains intact. I guide the group in reflecting on the light of the candle, to consider and discover their own metaphors of renewal and faith that it inspires. You may use a single candle or a full complement of candles in a *chanukiah*, the special holiday *menorah*.

The anticipated image-making is often to create a *menorah*, so if that is your intention ask participants ahead of time to bring found/natural/recyclable objects to share with others for their creations. In addition, provide clay, paints and decorative elements.

Tu B'Shvat

Tu B'shvat, the fifteenth of the month of *Shvat*, is called the New Year of the Trees. Its origin in the Torah was a time of renewal of our commitment to God in sharing the yield of the land with the poor. "Every year you shall set aside a tenth of the yield, so that you may learn to revere your God forever" (Deuteronomy 14:22-23). The medieval mystics of Safed carried *Tu B'shvat* a step further. For them trees symbolized humans – "For a human is like a tree of the field" (Deuteronomy 20:19). In line with their general concern for repair of the world – *tikkun olam* – the eating of a variety of fruits was a way to improve themselves spiritually.

Judaism's teaching on ecology assumes the human being is the guardian rather than the master of creation. God created the world and made human beings partners in the work of creation (Sabbath 10a) by appointing them guardians of his world (Genesis 2:16). As stewards, human beings are obliged to minimize wanton damage or destruction. According to *midrash*, God warned Adam and Eve that unless people protect the environment, leave it unprotected or destroy it, it will not be restored.

"When the Holy One, blessed be he, created the first man, He took him and led him around all the trees in the Garden of Eden and said to him: 'Behold My works, how beautiful and commendable they are. All that I have created, I have created for your sake. Be careful not to corrupt or destroy my world; for if you corrupt it, there will be no one after you to repair it.'" (*Midrash* Ecclesiastes viii: 12.1). The care of God's world is embodied in the commandment of *baltashchit*, no wanton destruction. It expresses an ethical concern for preservation and maintenance of the quality of the environment in the present and for future generations.

In Israel today, thousands of children plant trees and play a vital role in the improvement of our land. But, in recent decades, with global ecological crises looming, *Tu B'shvat* calls on us to take action against the willful and negligent devastation of God's world. Each of us must annually renew our commitment to do our part, individually and collectively as guardians, to allow nature to continue to inspire joy and awe.

For the other creative modalities, I may select for the meditation a chant: "*Ma gadlu ma'asechah Adonai, me'odam kumach'shevotecha*" –"How great are your works, Lord, How Profound is your design" (Psalm 92). For movement I encourage swaying and dancing like trees, feeling that you embody and are at one with the trees of the field. In the journaling part I ask participants to focus on nature and their various connections to it, perhaps describe a favorite place and its effect on you.

I would like to share some of my students' reflections on *Tu B'Shvat*:

Dahlia: "I had no clue what I was going to do. I'm no artist, and the idea of doing what I wanted scared me. As a preparatory exercise, the facilitator led us through a meditation. In the meditation, she told us to imagine a tree. A tree we felt comfortable by, a tree we had a relationship with. And suddenly my entire picture was in my mind very clearly. I've never experienced something like it. I knew what I was going to draw from beginning to end. When I opened my eyes, it was as if I was on a mission. I worked fast to accomplish my goal and wouldn't let anything stop me. I had a vision to carry out. I had a picture to draw!"

Rolinda: "We are, each of us, a Tree of Life, our roots planted deep in the life and soil of this and, our many branches reaching up to heaven, embracing one another with strength."

The sap of life runs through us. Our leaves are green, powered by photosynthesis, a gift from the sun...

I am tall and full

My moon cycles have waned, but new trees are coming, babies on the horizon.

There have been storms, fear, destruction, but I have weathered that, Baruch Hashem.

I love to dance when the wind moves me – wind / ruach / spirit

I love to nestle into the earth. It was always my dream to be planted in this land, in peace, and so it is. I am the Tree of Life and all who hold onto me are supported, upright. My paths are pleasant; they all lead to peace.

Rolinda – "The Tree of Life"

Purim

The story of *Purim* is apocryphal and takes place in a mythical kingdom outside of the Land of Israel. We read *Megillat Esther*, the Scroll of Esther, with all in the congregation adorned in costume and full of merriment. It is a fanciful story of potential persecution, heroism and rescue.

The spirit of *Purim* can best be captured in the Talmudic dictum: "A person is obligated to get spiced (drunk) on *Purim* until he does not know the difference between "Cursed be Haman and Blessed be Mordecai, *Arur Haman V'baruch Mordecai* " (*Megillat Esther* 7b). It calls on us to give free rein to our personalities signified by the phrase, *Ad Lo Yada*, until you no longer know, a state of drunkenness and blissful ignorance of reality, when all our inhibitions are swept away. On the other hand, *Ad Lo Yada* can also be considered as a higher degree of consciousness. It is a mystical moment when there is no difference between Mordecai and Haman, good and evil, for both are found in the Holy One who created light and darkness, made peace and created evil (Isaiah 45:7).

The Talmud goes on to say that it is only on *Purim* that we fully accept the Torah, for if we can make fun of our tradition, we are able to fully embrace and accept it. The joyous breaking of bounds is particularly important for adults, who usually feel constrained from acting out, playing or just having fun which come so naturally to us as children. So, on *Purim*, we have license to let out our repressed feelings as we overturn the rules. Anything goes. The crazier, the better.

We need Purim to laugh at what we most value, and to laugh at ourselves. This is a very important therapeutic process in which we have the opportunity to reflect on who we are, gain perspective and a true sense of self, and are encouraged to mock it. So, it's a time to feel good, let loose and masquerade – a sense of fantasy and imagi-nation reign.

In Expressive Kavannah, I like to make and use masks at *Pu-rim*. Making molds of our faces allows us to reflect on who we are, to conceal that person and become another personality inspired by our imagination. Masks permit the person to hide their own face/person-ality and take on a new one. Even though the observer knows this is a masquerade, in the spirit of *Purim*, she plays along with the game.

In practice, the making of plaster masks require rolls of gauze/ plaster (like for making a cast) and Vaseline petroleum jelly. Working in pairs, one person smears the partner's face with Vaseline, then covers the face with wet plaster strips, leaving holes for the nostrils, eyes and mouth. After several layers the strips will start to harden and soon are able to be removed. Then the partners switch roles. After getting over the initial discomfort, the process of having one's face covered affords each person with an opportunity to enter into deep introspection on who they are. We follow by a journaling period to capture the insights gained.

The second session continues after the plaster has dried, at least overnight or a few days later. With the insights gained in the first part of the process, we then add the magic of imagination and create our *Purim* personality, painting and decorating the masks and assembling them into imaginative costumes and acting out our fantasies. Expressing her readiness to be spontaneous and trust the process, Luisa stated: "My favorite class was probably the mask-making, I liked the messiness and the fact that it was a medium that I was not used to...I just let my creativity go for it."

I usually document this workshop with photographs, reflecting the sheer fun of exploring a medium that is different and messy. The students take pleasure in the whimsical nature of the process as preparation for the craziness of Purim.

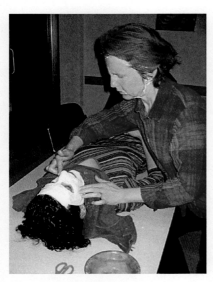

Jean making a plaster mask on Lindy

Rolinda dancing with her mask

Edna and Pardes students with masks   Photo: Debbi Cooper

Passover

Pessach, Passover, the celebration of the Exodus from Egypt is a spring holiday with both historical and agricultural antecedents. The predominant mood is joy and celebration, of the barley harvest and of freedom. At this time of year, families gather together at the *Seder* table to read the *Haggadah*, literally "the telling," to pass on from generation to generation the story of the Exodus. "For a seven-day period, you shall eat *matzot*...for a strong hand removed you from Egypt. You shall observe this decree at its designated time from year to year" (Exodus 13:6-10). Each year as we relive the Exodus, we discover new meanings gleaned from our individual experiences which enrich and place ourselves in the narrative. God reveals his love for the children of Israel by bringing them out of Egypt as a newly birthed people, from slavery to freedom, from darkness to light.

In addition to the *Haggadah*, we read *Shir Hashirim*, the biblical Song of Songs, which some view as a metaphor for the love between God and Israel before their wedding journey across the sea "on the wings of eagles" (Exodus 19:4). Song of Songs enjoins us "not to awaken love before it pleases" referring to *Pessach* as a time of love for God. We extend this Divine love to our fellow Jews in the spring, a time of renewal.

My peak experience of teaching Passover was in 1998, when a group of eight women joined me on a three-day Expressive Kavannah retreat to the Sinai desert (now a part of Egypt) in preparation for the holiday. We explored several different concepts in the Passover story all of which in themselves may be a focus for a class or workshop: the slavery/freedom duality; the journey of the children of Israel from *Mitzraim*, Egypt, derived from the Hebrew word *tsar*, narrow, and corresponding to the narrow strip of fertility on either side of the Nile River; on the ancient plagues or on those more contemporary, such as carbon pollution, acidification of oceans and waters, loss of biodiversity and poverty; or our own personal paths into places of constriction, addiction or slavery and our own liberation.

As Rabbi Richard Levy teaches in his *Haggadah*, <u>On Wings of Freedom</u>:

"*Mitzrayim* is not just a place on an ancient map
Where a narrow strait blocks the way between two seas,
Mitzrayim is a place in us,
Where a narrow strait blocks the Sea which is our soul
From reaching the Sea which is its source".

In Sinai we looked at and played with the concept of *mezuzah*, which first appears in the biblical account of the Exodus from Egypt as the sign written in blood by the children of Israel on their doorposts to keep the forces of death and destruction away from their homes while the Egyptian first born were slaughtered. The Torah says: "And they shall take of the blood and they shall put it on the two mezuzot (doorposts) and on the lintel... For the Lord will pass through to smite the Egyptians, and when He sees the blood upon the lintel, and on the two doorposts, the Lord will pass over the door, and He will not allow the destroyer to come in unto your houses to smite [you]" (Exodus 12:7 and 23). This is why the Holiday of the Exodus is called Passover. Until this day Jews everywhere place a *mezuzah* on the doors of their homes in the belief that it has the power to protect us.

Today, the *mezuzah* serves as the symbol of a Jewish home. Upon every entry or exit, many still kiss the *mezuzah* to remind them of their covenant with God. The covenant from Deuteronomy is inscribed on the parchment inside the *mezuzah's* case (Deuteronomy 6:4-9, 11:13-21) and the word *Shaddai* (*shin-dalet-yod*) or just its first letter *shin* is written on the outer casing: "*Shomer Delatot Israel*"– Protect the Doors of Israel.

As the activities of the Expressive Kavannah retreat in Sinai took place over several days, we engaged in many different activities and modalities to both appreciate our awesome natural surroundings and engage with evocative *Pessach* themes. Here are several examples to use in workshops or classes. One activity is to devote the image-making to creating *mezuzot*. The outer casing has no specifications except for the *shin or shadai*. It can be clay, wood or any other material and decorated to each person's taste. The inside scroll can be added later, or you may prepare copies for everyone to use. On the retreat we wrote our own prayers.

Appropriately enough, our movement was inspired by dancing at the Red Sea. Our intention was to relive Exodus 15:20 – "Miriam, the prophetess...took her drum in her hand and all the women went forth after her with drums and with dances." Dancing needs room so if you have an outdoor space and can even provide instruments, that's perfect.

The retreat group decided that the appropriate culmination for our journey was physically crossing back over the Egyptian-Israeli border with *kavannah*. After all the necessary passport formalities, we gathered to walk silently across the border.

Shavuot

Shavuot is the culmination of our festival cycle symbolizing revelation, spiritual elevation and reception, *kabbalah*.

On the second night of Pessach we commence a counting, known as the *Omer*, a 49-day, seven week journey that leads us to *Shavuot*, literally Festival of the Weeks, which celebrates the revelation of Torah at Sinai. In biblical times, the counting was connected to agriculture; at *Pessach* the barley ripened and at *Shavuot*, the spring wheat. Therefore, the celebration was known as the Feast of the Harvest (Exodus 23: 14-19) or the Day of the First Fruits (Leviticus 23: 9-22).

As they did for much of normative Jewish practice, the great medieval mystics of the *Kabbalah* transformed the holiday by attributing this time to the receiving of Torah at Sinai. The *Zohar*, the most important Jewish mystical book, describes *Shavuot* as a day of mystical union between the feminine aspect of God – the *Shechinah* and the masculine. The imagery is that of a wedding between God and the Jewish people.

The counting of the *Omer* helps us retrace our steps from slavery to freedom. On *Pessach* our intention is to re-experience slavery and redemption. On *Shavuot*, we celebrate revelation, honoring our receiving of Torah at Sinai through our remembrance that "the soul of every Jew" was gathered at the base of the mountain as witnesses to this miraculous event.

Revelation, unlike any other form of communication, is experienced outside any known framework of everyday space and time. In each generation revelation continues to flourish within us as we learn, teach, experience and interact with others, with our environment and with God. This life-long unfolding process must be transformed into action, as well as the basis for accessing our higher selves. If we remain open and receptive, *Shechinah* speaks to each of us in different ways and at different times. The Torah renews our lives.

I like to lead a visualization mediation for *Shavuot*. "See yourself standing with the multitudes at the foot of the mountain. Hear the sounds of thunderous *shofar* blasts in anticipation of Moses' return with the two inscribed tablets. Experience the energy of truth emerging into your consciousness. Sense yourself open, ready and willing to receive."

What did you hear? The whole of the Ten Commandments, the first two, only the first word "*Anochi*", "I am" from *"Anochi Adonai Elochecha"*, "I am the Lord, your God."

Thomas – inspired by Reb Nachman

Another meditation is to focus on the letter *aleph*, **א**, which is the first letter of the Ten Commandments. *Aleph* has no sound. "See the letter, hear the sound of its mysterious silence and let it unfold for you into image, dance and poetry."

For image-making include Hebrew newspapers or magazines for inclusion of the letters in their work, in addition to the usual array of media. A group movement activity might be dancing together, as if at Sinai preparing to receive Torah. Imagine the experience at Sinai in a poem, again use the Haiku format.

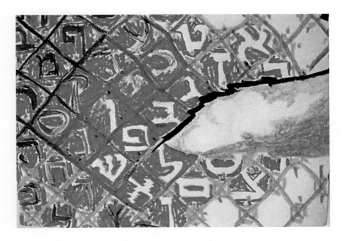

Jean – "Flying Carpet"

According to Dr. Michael Kagan: "The cycle of the Jewish year can be viewed and lived as a healing spiral. Each festival interweaves with the one before and the one after it to create a truly holistic journey...the cycle forms an organic whole. Wholeness is a criterion for holiness, and holism bridges the gap between the two."

8

TORAH PORTIONS
TEXT TO TEXTURE

The Torah, the Five Books of Moses, has a wealth of stories, situations, themes and metaphors to draw upon for learning, reflection, insight and creativity. A portion of the Torah is read every *Shabbat* along with a selection from prophetic literature, the *Haftorah*, that relates in some way to it. These prophetic readings may also offer a range of additional material well suited to stimulate producing imagery, as well as development of each student's intentionality and personal interpretation in relation to the text.

For ongoing classes, the weekly readings essentially provide a cohesive, integrated thematic framework. My own understanding of the human creative process is deeply influenced by the grand Creation myth from the first Torah portion itself, *Bereshit*, "In the Beginning". As part of the story, humans are made in the image of God, and therefore each of us carries within innate creative potential.

In this section, I have chosen to share a number of portions, offering how, what and why I select certain aspects of particular portions to transmit in the Jewish learning component of Expressive Kavannah. In reading the biblical narrative, not just as a story, but to get a sense of general themes, I search for metaphors or concepts connected to contemporary life. It could be a universal theme that resonates for me and hopefully others. Often, my choices are based on my own learning, what images strike me intuitively and what I truly enjoy teaching. If you enjoy and relate to the material personally, you will be able to teach in a much more exciting and evocative manner.

As a prelude to teaching others, I consider what the concept "struggle", for example, is for me: Why do I struggle? What do I struggle against? How does it make me feel? What process do I go through? What do I learn from it? I believe each person can benefit from reflection and introspection. Healing comes from expressing our issues in many different ways: discussion, writing, meditation, or image-making. Taking participants through their own experiences of struggle, or whatever concept is selected, can be of therapeutic value.

Before teaching a given Torah portion, I re-read it and ask that my students do so as well in preparation for the class. Whether students study in advance is always a dilemma for teachers in any setting, so don't count too heavily on it depending on the circumstances, ongoing class, retreat or a one-timer. I try to approach the text with fresh eyes each time I teach as I am also changing and learning from year to year. I feel blessed by gleaning new insights that present new aspects and interpretations to impart.

I endeavor to facilitate my students moving from "text to texture". Jewish learning is usually very cerebral, an abstract intellectual pursuit to interpret text. Producing personal, concrete images supports both intellectual memory and deepens meaning. Images created usually reflect individual interpretations filtered through personal history. Each person has a different perspective of what is meaningful. For example, when studying the text of a Torah portion as a point of departure, I weave in creative experimentation, rather than student's day-to-day intellectual discussions. I encourage students to explore the associations with the biblical narrative as a metaphor for personal issues.

In observing my students make the transition from studying a Torah portion to creative endeavors, I am always amazed as their images emerge. They capture what the words can't and become themselves *midrash*, an interpretive comment on the Torah.

Lech Lecha (Genesis 12:1-3)

Lech Lecha is the story of Avram (later Abraham) hearing the call and leaving the land of his ancestors and journeying to the land which he will be shown by God. In *Lech Lecha*: "Now the Lord said to Avram, Go for yourself from your land, from your relatives, and from your father's house to the land that I will show you. And I will make of you a great nation; I will bless you, and make your name great, and you shall be a blessing."

In teaching *Lech Lecha*, I may choose to focus on certain issues, such as leaving home, hearing a spiritual call, being tested by one's faith, rebellion, or idol worship. While the selection might at first be somewhat arbitrary, in my own review I seek out ideas that I believe will strike an emotional, psychological or spiritual response, stimulate the imagination and relate to something for me personally. All of us have left our parents' home, or our children have left us, and each of us carries feelings around that process, whether smooth or fraught with conflict.

Jo – "*Lech Lecha*"

If I choose to focus on the call, I direct my teaching to encourage the group to enter the space of experiencing a personal
spiritual call. Critical to the story is the challenging spiritual journey
that Avram embarked upon without knowing the outcome. I emphasize that aspect as a metaphor for how we all are challenged by
life and how we deal with our own struggles. I want participants to
feel how they too may have been tested in life, to venture into the
unknown, to trust in the journey as a process of growth. To meet
critical life challenges requires the utmost faith and courage and the
images evoked may assist us in the process. Avram's transformation
is complete when even his name is changed to Abraham.

Another potential focus might be on how "blessing" fits into a
student's personal experience. Each of us has come to believe or not,
to select particular spiritual practices, and each of us desires that our
unique spiritual paths will as with Avram end in a blessing.

I encourage students to consider the call in several different
ways each of which are stimulated by the fascinating reflexive gram-
matical formulation of the words, *Lech Lecha* – go by yourself; go to
yourself; go inward to find your inner truth; or get on with it, that
is do what you came to do. All offer rich material for meditation and
imagery.

As elaborated in the chapter on meditation, I try to make
a connection between the meditation, both in technique and content, and the learning, to enable a smooth transition to the image-making. In the case of *Lech Lecha*, I may choose the word *bracha*, blessing as a seed thought or to personalize Avram's challenge
I may combine two types of meditations. First, a silent walking
meditation which supports a bodily experience of the journey. The
slow, deliberate movement deepens and reinforces the emotional
and spiritual experience. Then, a guided sitting meditation using *bracha*, or even the reflexive words *Lech Lecha*, (*Lechi Lach* is the
feminine form), as a seed thought. I start with a few words as they

close their eyes: "Connect with God and use the metaphor in the portion for your own spiritual and creative journey. Know that it requires
faith and courage. Believe in something that gives your life more
meaning and imagine expressing it. Physical change opens you to
new possibilities. Change is felt on many different levels. Keep *bracha* in your consciousness. Let it unfold for you now. Be aware
of how you sense it, see it and where it takes you."

Vayeira (Genesis 18 -22)

Tamara – "*Vayeira*"

Vayeira is well known for the Binding of Isaac, called the
Akeidah in Hebrew. The opening scene is Abraham sitting outside of
his tent. "God appeared to him in the plains of the Mamre while he
was sitting at the entrance to his tent." (18:1).

At times I have chosen to focus my teaching on this opening scene with Abraham sitting, or meditating, and the appearance
of God soon after. Not only do I personally relate to meditation,
but students will experience a taste of it immediately following the

teaching component. The act of meditating, or sitting, stilling ourselves gives an enormous resource of serenity and depth. If we are
made in the image of God, then we ourselves have the potentialities
of consciousness, to be serene and deep. Our connection with God is
then the inspiration for our creativity, we make the connection between *emunah*, faith and *omanut*, art.

In another part of the story Sarah is promised a son in her
old age. What is her reaction? She laughs: "God has made laughter
for me, whoever hears will laugh for me" (21:6). Not only is the word
"laughter" the basis of naming their son "Itzhak" (my father's name),
but here the word "edna", the source of my name, is introduced.
"Edna" is a *hapax legomenon*, a word that only appears only once in
the Torah. Its meaning is therefore left to personal interpretation, according to the context. It conjures up the idea of pleasure or rejuve-
nation, old people finding pleasure in the most unlikely places. In any
case the idea of names holding particular meanings can be a focus
for subsequent meditation and imagery.

Sarah's pleasure stands in stark contrast to the dramatic
scene of the Binding of Isaac, *the Akeidah*. Starting in *Lech Lecha*,
Abraham was tested being asked to leave his homeland and family to
prove his faith in God. Here again he is being tested, a major theme
in the portion, "God tested Abraham" (22:1).

The *midrashic* interpretation considers "tested" in two different ways. It could be related to the word miracle (*nisa – nes*). So, we
could understand that God exalted Abraham, trial upon trial, so he
could achieve his potential. Or that God's motivation was to have
Abraham fear Him.

In presenting this portion, I may also focus the learning on
the very concept of contrast itself. Doing so I point out the main
themes in the narrative of love, laughter, hope as opposed to destruction, testing and sacrifice in the stories of Abraham, Sarah and
Isaac. I reverse the order of events in the portion, starting with the

notion of sacrifice first, *Akeidah*, and ending with the notion of pleasure, *edna*. My intention in this approach is for the group to experience these events as separate and then in contrast to each other, imagining the scenes and the emotions tied to each one. Reliving, imagining and reframing one's life events in the image-making may offer renewed strength to deal with the difficulties of life.

I select this thematic framework to stimulate personal imaginary scenes of father or a mother, especially in the case of an all-women's group, being asked to sacrifice her only child, whether literally or metaphorically. Then similar to the walking meditation I may use in *Lech Lecha*, I ask students to split into pairs and bind one another's hands with string to make the experience immediate and vivid.

Tamara's poem "Response to the *Akeidah*"

No way
could I plunge dagger to heart
my own flesh
Sooner would I melt
into silent oblivion
torn by tears
that will not cease

For a meditative theme, I may guide them to focus on sacrifice and/or pleasure in their lives, to find hope in challenging situations and access the power to shape our own attitudes and our lives. The Jewish mystical tradition teaches that much of what is experienced in daily existence stems from our own attitudes and desires. We are advised that, in countless ways, both discernable and hidden, each of our acts, words, and even thoughts leave its indelible imprint on the universe. "Everything is dependent on man's free will. In truth, a man by his actions is always drawing to himself to good or evil, according to the path which he treads. The Maggid of Mezritch, the chief disciple of the Baal Shem Tov, once declared: "Each person creates his own Paradise."

In psychological terms this is called "reframing". Seeing a situation from a different point of view, so as to act on it and change our attitude towards it. We can permit ourselves to make choices that empower us. Use your imagination to the fullest to visualize your own Paradise on earth. This image could be one you can access whenever you are in a situation where you need it.

Vayishlach (Genesis 28:10-15)

The portion opens with the presence of angels as the messengers of God. *Vayishlach* illustrates Jacob's psychological and spiritual development in the biblical narrative. In my teaching, I refer to fundamental processes of growth and development that characterize human life: the transformation of a human being from an egocentric, unconscious person to one of wholeness, vision and spiritual awareness. My intention is to enhance each one's understanding of their own personal growth and transformation throughout their lives.

Four basic experiences change and transform Jacob so fundamentally that even his name changes from Jacob to *"Yisrael"*, one who wrestles with the divine. Jacob's first experience is suffering. When he robs his brother of his father's blessing for his first born, Esau becomes enraged and vows to kill him. "The time to mourn for my father will soon be here. Then I will kill my brother Jacob" (27: 41). Jacob's failure to anticipate his brother's anger causes him great anguish, so he flees into the wilderness, embarking on a frightening and painful journey.

Jacob's second experience is his encounter with the Divine. In the depths of the night Jacob dreams of a ladder with angels reaching from heaven to earth. God speaks to him directly saying: "I am God, the God of Abraham your father and God of Isaac" (28:13).

Upon awakening he declares: "Surely God is in this place and I did not know" (28:16). The dream and spiritual encounter come to Jacob precisely at the moment of his own psychological crisis.

Leah – "*Vayishlach, Surely God is in this Place*"

The third great event is Jacob falling in love with Rachel. It is one of the great love stories of the Bible. The transition from the world of childhood to world of adulthood is a universal rite-of-passage.

The fourth major event in *Vayishlach* has Jacob taking responsibility for his past deeds and seeking reconciliation with Esau. God commands him to return to the land of his fathers. Jacob shows spiritual maturity by trusting God with a new, open, honest and direct relationship with God. "For I have seen the Divine face to face –"*panim el panim*" (32:31). He now has to face his brother alone which takes spiritual courage.

Alone at night by the side of the stream Jabbok there was a man, *ish*, (32:25) who wrestled with him until daybreak. Jacob refused to break it off until he understood its meaning. "Your name shall no longer be Jacob, but *Yisrael*, because you have struggled with God and overcome" (32:29). The name change reflects a metamorphosis of his inner nature. His struggle with God reveals the actualization of his spiritual potential. I find the essence of the encounter in the struggle itself and its purpose to test or challenge Jacob in a way that would lead him to fundamental transformation. All of us may at one time or another confront a spiritual challenge, or an inner struggle. Whether we are able to emerge changed, transformed, or reborn is dependent on our willingness to confront it.

The final test for Jacob comes in the confrontation with his brother Esau. The two brothers embrace and weep, their tears evidence of their forgiveness and acceptance of one another. Jacob's destiny has been fulfilled, he has reconciled with himself, with God and with Esau.

There are many metaphors in Jacob's story which can be selected as a focus for teaching, meditation and image-making: the wilderness experience; strength and courage; the spiritual encounter; God-wrestling; purpose; self-fulfillment; and the one I really enjoy teaching, the change of name and personal identity that reflects the metamorphosis of Jacob's, *Yisrael's* inner nature. In selecting a focus for the meditation, I usually choose to emphasize the process of becoming spiritually, psychologically and emotionally aware. Perhaps everyone who is called upon to a higher psychological development must undergo a wilderness experience. There are many ways we are subjected to undertake such a journey. It can take the form of a period of doubt, anxiety, a grave sickness or depression. These are very difficult situations, but we cannot eliminate the suffering, as we have to have the courage to confront it, to give a voice to it, and to find a form in which it can be expressed so in the end we realize transformation and healing.

The process of spiritual development is something we each have experienced in very personal ways. We receive "inner messages" in the form of dreams, intuition or coincidences daily. Our job is to pay attention to them and so they can lead us to a place of wholeness. So, the meditation can be a visualization, such as having people imagine a place or a situation of a "wilderness experience" where they had these kinds of dreams or intuitions.

B'Shallach (Exodus 13:17-22)

B'Shallach contains the well-known story of the Exodus in which God parts the Red Sea – the Jews are saved, the Egyptians drown. Every year at Passover, Jews the world over tell and re-tell the story from generation to generation. The uplifting, hopeful and miraculous salvation of the Jewish people is expressed in the poem "Song of the Sea", Shirat Hayam, an inspirational piece of literature also known as the "Poem of Praise." All of Shirat Hayam is rich with vivid, stimulating images, so there is a wide range of choice. I have chosen a few verses to illustrate the words that evoke the anger, war, death, destruction and finally, salvation with Miriam leading the women in song and dance.

3   "God is Master of War, His name is God…
4   Pharaoh's chariots and army He threw into the sea, and the pick of his officers were mired in the Sea of Reeds…
8   At a blast from Your nostrils the waters were heaped up; straight as a wall stood the running water, the deep waters congealed in the heart of the sea…
18 The Lord reigns For ever…
19 When Pharaoh's horses, chariots and horsemen went into the sea, the Lord brought the waters of the sea back over them, but the Israelites walked through the sea on dry ground…

20 Then Miriam the prophet, Aaron's sister, took a timbrel in her hand, and all the women followed her, with timbrels and dancing. 21 Miriam sang to them: Sing to the Lord, for he is highly exalted Both horse and driver, He has hurled into the sea"

A story of miracles, Exodus, *Yitziyat Mitzraim*, literally means "coming out of Egypt". By liberating the Children of Israel from enslavement, God reveals his love for Israel as a newly birthed people. *Mitzraim*, Egypt, is derived from the word *tsar* which means narrow. Egypt therefore can be seen not only as the physically narrow strip of fertility along the Nile bordered by desert wilderness, but also metaphorically the narrow place in us, constriction in our psyches that blocks our potential. Each of us may feel constricted or enslaved by our addictions, whether to substances, consumerism, the internet, TV, or the daily grind of work that gives little or no satisfaction. So too, we are responsible for breaking free or remaining enslaved, and we make the choice every day.

You can choose to focus your teaching on the role of Miriam, the priestess, who exhibits courage and strength in leading the women and children of Israel across the sea. Alternatively, you might also choose to focus on the roles of Moses, the redeemer, or on Pharaoh, the omnipotent enslaver. With an intention to guide students to feel the story personally, I often remind them that each of us can choose to see within both the liberator and the one with a hardened heart, indifferent to others suffering. By looking inside, we can explore two juxtaposed concepts: enslavement and joy. We may be the cause of our own constriction by our attitudes, habits and unawareness of others and ourselves. Joy emerges only when we free ourselves to access the joy in our hearts.

For the meditation I often use the uplifting words of the great Hassidic rabbi, Nachman of Bretzlav, "*Kol ha'olam gesher tsar me'od ve'ha'ikar lo le'fahed clal* – The whole world is a narrow bridge and the essence is not to be afraid at all." First singing, then humming, and then silently. The inherent idea in these words is that we can overcome our struggles with courage and faith. It is within our power to free ourselves from our constrictions to touch the joy within us.

Yitro (Exodus 18:1- 20:23)

Yitro contains one of the most important and dramatic events in the Torah: the giving of the Ten Commandments to the people of Israel at Mount Sinai. In preparation for receiving the Torah, God reminds Moses "You have seen what I did to Egypt, and that I have borne you on the wings of eagles and brought you to Me. And now... if you will obey Me faithfully and keep My covenant, you will be My treasured possession among all the peoples. Indeed, all the earth is Mine, but you shall be to Me a kingdom of priests and a holy nation" (Exodus 19:5-6).

According to the story, divine revelation was experienced by multitudes at the foot of the mountain in the presence of God, God's voice emanating from on high accompanied by thunder, lightning, smoke and fire to the blasts of the shofar. God spoke to the Jewish people, giving them the Ten Commandments. Commentators say the people actually heard the first two and Moses taught them the other eight.

The first five of the Ten Commandments address God-human relationships. The first three commandments ask for our acceptance of God. The first relates to having faith in God's existence as eternal (Exodus 20:2). The second relates to not having any other Gods (Exodus 20:3-6). The third teaches that it is forbidden to use God's name in vain. The fourth commandment requires us to remember (zachor) and observe (shmor) the Sabbath. The fifth commandment requires us to honor our parents (Exodus 20:12), as our tradition and the Torah hold dear our connection to successive generations.

The last five commandments are about relationships between

human beings. The sixth commandment states the prohibition of murder. Here it acts as a guide to encourage moral behavior. The seventh commandment prohibits committing adultery; the eighth prohibits stealing. The ninth commandment prohibits bearing false witness against a fellow man, included in this is also slander and gossip. The tenth commandment prohibits envy of what others have. Appreciating what we have is the sign of humility.

In conclusion, Rav Kook considers these precepts as aspiration to fulfill our purpose as a Holy Nation by embodying our higher selves. Our task is both external and internal. On the one hand, we teach others to be moral and on the other we are called to focus inwardly tending to our own spiritual growth.

In my teaching of *Yitro*, I strive to go beyond comprehending Ten Commandments from an intellectual point of view. However, experiencing them in Expressive Kavannah provides a very different perspective: one of exploration through meditation and the arts using our intuition and imagination to reveal the purpose and meaning of the commandments in our lives.

For meditation, I like to use a chant using the first commandment: "*Anochi Adonai Elochecha* – I am *Adonai*, your God.*" The chant can be sung all together, then slowly hummed, and finally be internalized. When ready, participants can move into image-making. Alternatively, you can let the participants choose the commandment they most relate to. They can then use a word from it as a seed thought for meditation. This could be very meaningful for some to consider what the commandment means to them. Using another technique, the whole biblical description of the giving of the tablets at Mount Sinai is full of very powerful imagery which can be used as a visualization, either seeing oneself standing at Sinai or of imagining the scene. Any of these different approaches will provide an impetus for the mediation and later engage the imagination.

Mina – "Israel receiving Torah at Sinai"

As participants emerge from meditation which has stimulated flow, they transition fluidly into image-making. This means their concepts will become images which are then visible to them for contemplation. These in turn will provide inspiration for music, dance and creative writing. The experience of working subconsciously with the arts may reveal deeper understandings of themselves.

I enjoy teaching this portion because of its centrality and importance in laying the foundations of Judaism – God's oneness. By embracing this concept, we accept being bound to follow the code of morality which was revealed to govern our daily lives. We can access this spiritual stance daily through awareness, prayer, meditation and gratitude. *Yitro* also clarifies important values for many of us. For example, recognizing the fifth commandment, "honor your father and mother" may influence some to reconcile with their parents following disputes. We are given opportunities every day to consider our relationships with others and decide whether and how to act, who we are and who we want to be.

9

JOURNEYS

This chapter gives voice to my students' stories of Expressive Kavannah. Some of them have worked with me over many years. Their impressions are invaluable to me as their feedback keeps me on track. Their suggestions and critiques help me to change and develop my teaching. I learn from my students as they learn from me. I feel fortunate for this enriching experience.

Margaret

I would like to dedicate this chapter to Margaret Gottstein (*z"l*, of blessed memory) who passed away in April 2014 at the age of 87. Margaret was one of my longest standing students, having worked with me for some 15 years. An accomplished artist, Margaret loved the spirituality and spontaneity of the method in addition to the supportive and validating group she was part of. During her last year, she claimed that this was the only activity she looked forward to all week. I miss her and cherish her memory.

Margaret has an interesting history which is worth sharing. Margaret Hannah Pincus was born in 1926 in Melbourne, Australia. The family followed her dentist father, Paul Pincus, when he relocated to England 1936-1947. (Paul served in the medical corps of the British army and her mother, Myrtle, served in the Red Cross during the war. Her elder brother, John, was shot down over France fighting the Nazis). She told funny family stories about the blitz. To her children, it seemed incredible that there should be anything funny about that time in London but apart from when she was sent to the countryside to be out of harm's way, all her wartime stories were accompanied by her laughing her head off and grinning as she told them.

At age 21, she studied art in France for a year. The family relocated again back to Australia where she married Frank Gottstein (1924-1997) and had two children, Ian (1962-2002) and Helen (1964-). In 1992, Frank and she moved to Jerusalem to be close to her grandchildren. She wanted, she said, "to be part of the furniture of their lives."

Margaret continued to love art, Australia, birds and nature in general. She was instrumental in creating the Merri Creek inner city park lands in Melbourne and in Jerusalem, she volunteered for many years at the Hanson garden and brought nature and dirt under fingernails to hundreds of volunteers.

Margaret's experience with Expressive Kavannah was very important to her. She had a space to practice her art within a supportive group. She once revealed to me that "I create a space with no fear of criticism." This was liberation for her as traditional art classes are very judgmental. She loved to create to music and her work reflected that mood. Also, a nature lover, she often painted outside where she was in her element. And joining Kehilat Kol Haneshama in Jerusalem after immigrating to Israel, she developed an interest in Jewish learning.

As an older person I was very pleased with her willingness to share her most personal experiences reflected in her work. A multi-faceted person, we all learned much from her.

Margaret – "Frank's Death"

The moment of Frank's death.
The black is this world, the blue is the world to come,
and the gap is the moment when he changed from one
to the other

Margaret – "Mountains at Eilat"

Mountains at Eilat, the feeling they give of being close to God.
In the foreground – me and Frank's shadow.
I cried at Eilat, it was so full of his presence for me.

Rolinda

Rolinda always remembers her first class with me at The Pardes Institute of Jewish Studies in Jerusalem in 1999, the year her father died. The class was a preparation for *Rosh Hashana* and a verse spontaneously appeared on her page: "*Kaddish* is an Aramaic marathon race and a man always gets to the finish line first..."

Rolinda is a dancer, writer and Breema practitioner. Being married to a rabbi, she is well versed in Jewish studies and texts and has experienced eclectic forms of *davening* (praying) in synagogues in the US and Israel.

As a dancer, she loved taking our meditations into space: stretching, feeling the energy build, then flowing into the creative zone free of tension and stress, free to express whatever was inside her without planning, without criticism, with creative joy.

As a writer, she dove into the journaling as an opportunity to record her life. She kept her very full journal over many years in class. She would often share entries from the previous years inspired by the same *parshah* saying "I am in a different place today!" She wrote poems sparked by our meditations and image-making on the backs of her pieces. She claimed her poems often incorporated images that she might not otherwise have accessed. She felt that some of the images were "core" to her being and soul mission.

When we began to create collages made of found materials and magazines, she would find printed words to glue onto the images. I taught the students to turn a creation upside down to see it from a different perspective. New meaning would reveal itself from this practice. Many of her recent pieces are taped to the wall of her study. "I see them every day, and though I no longer remember the prompts and meditations that created them, they represent core parts of my recent past".

She felt her inner experience of the upcoming Torah portion or holiday was deepened by the Expressive Kavannah journey, and often would bring her art piece to her family's Shabbat table to illustrate her *dvar Torah*, interpretations and insightful lunderstandings of the holiday or Torah portion of the week. In our classes over the years, she shared the joy of becoming a grandmother for the first time, the sadness of losing loved ones, including a beloved member of our class, the anguish and challenges facing our people, our region, and the planet, and many pleasant hours spent enriching our inner and outer lives together.

She particularly enjoyed working creatively in small, non-judgmental, accepting groups. She says she remembers many of the pieces her classmates created and how they shared them with the group. "Each of us works in her own way, each different, each unique, springing from the same preparation in an entirely different direction." She said that Expressive Kavannah enriched and deepened her life, grateful for the womens' warmth and wisdoms harnessed by our groups over the years.

Rolinda – "In the heart of the *Mishkan*"

Rolinda – "Yom Hazikaron"

Amita

Amita is a woman in her mid-fifties. She originally came to Israel in her twenties and stayed for 6 years. During that period, she received a Physical Therapy degree from the University of Tel Aviv. Returning to the United States she received rabbinic ordination from the Reconstructionist Rabbinical College in Philadelphia. She acted as a full-time congregational rabbi in her native New England for five years, returning to Jerusalem where she worked as a physical therapist in nursing homes. She also trained in Chaplaincy and Spiritual Care.

Her primary mode of creative expression is dance. She loves

free, unstructured forms such as Five Rhythms, Open Floor, Contact Improvisation and Authentic Movement. She also loves to sing and has been a Cantor in Jewish religious services for twenty years, traveling to the States to participate in High Holiday services.

Amita first experienced Expressive Kavannah at an Interfaith Shavuot Retreat. An essential part of the retreat is all night study. My workshop did not start until 4:00 a.m. I instructed the participants to work with clay with eyes closed. Amita experienced it as a meditative process and was happy with the surprise result as an internal process with an external manifestation. For her, it was an important expression of what she was experiencing at that time immersed in this three-day retreat.

Consequently, I invited her to join my ongoing group which she came to feel was a significant piece of her life during that period. She loved working in silence for an hour in the company of other women also engaged in creative activity. The singing, dancing, and meditating supported her inner exploration and expression finding her own *kavannah*, as well as that of the others in the group.

The context of the classes usually focuses on the weekly Torah portion which I often teach as a metaphor for universal themes of life. Amita always goes beyond the literal text, applying the learning to confront her own issues, emotionaland spiritual.

The piece "Inner Mother and Child" was done after we studied the weekly Torah portion *VaEra* (Genesis 6-10). I asked the group to focus on their own *"mitzrayim"* (the Hebrew word for Egypt literally meaning "a narrow place", a place of constriction or difficulty). Focus on the place where they felt constricted and wanted to leave behind. Amita responded that she was coming out of a fundamental state of insecurity to a place she had discovered on the retreat where she could rest within herself. She felt she was able to hold the *kavannah* to stay relaxed and gentle with herself as she sculpted. She was in an altered state, totally absorbed, the work was itself a meditation. "It beautifully expressed the feeling of my inner mother holding my inner child." The sculpture she created amazed her.

Amita – "Inner Mother and Child"

After a lesson on the Torah portion *Shemot* (Exodus 1-6), I asked the participants to visualize the emotional colors of the week in their meditation. Amita saw the "Burning Bush" inside her with spaciousness inside and around the fire. A hurt and angry dragon shed tears, and then a rainbow came out of her, starting with angry black and red, flowing into more cheerful and calm colors.

Amita – "Dragon Tears"

A few days before Amita had received a rejection letter from a program she had anticipated participating in. She had been on a journey from hurt to anger burning in her all week. Then, after she looked at her work the anger dissipated into acceptance as she realized it was in her best interest not to go.

Mina

Mina is a mature woman in her seventies. A therapist, an activist, a sculptress and a very devoted grandmother. She puts all of herself into the activities she engages in. In joining Expressive Kavannah, she was most interested in acquiring expressivity and spontaneity in her work. She soon realized that it didn't need to be "representative", but "expressive". In these samples of her work over a period of years, she sees the changes both in her expressive quality paralleled with and her psychological development. A case in point are the following *Tu B'Shvat* projects done over three different years where she comments on the changes, she perceives both in what she refers to as "expanded creativity".

The first year, she painted a Redwood tree – very large and dark with a burnt-out hole at the bottom in which she sat hunched over with head in hands – a figure of sorrow and pain. The next *Tu B'Shvat* she painted a large tree growing out of two hills, or breasts, as a symbol of growing out of her heart. The tree was filled with branches and leaves and a nest with two birds as a sign of life and renewal.

The third year, she sculpted a tree incorporating a small broken tree branch. She expressed awareness of the progression over these three years of moving from a simple painting with lots of sorrow, to adding other materials and putting a more expanded outlook, to the final one which is sculpted and incorporating other materials and projecting a feeling of life and fertility. So, there are two progressions –one in subject matter and feelings expressed, and the other in the materials used and the expanded creativity.

Similarly, Mina created *Purim* masks each year over a period of three years. In the first one, she used a prepared mask and painted it red with black features and black beads for hair. This represented her darker side and a form of resistance to making a pretty mask.

A year later, she painted the face divided in half, one side colorful, pretty and happy and the other side black and ugly and chaotic representing both sides of herself. The third year she chose to use only black materials, which was actually beautiful and powerful – somehow overcoming the dichotomy between good and bad, ugly and beautiful.

"These projects are all consistent in the way they show my process emotionally and artistically over time. For me each project has been very satisfying to create, although in the early years I felt very critical of my limited artistic abilities. At this point, I've been freed to use whatever materials are available to actualize my starting image. I've allowed the materials to determine and alter my mental image with results that satisfy and often inspire me. I'm so grateful to Edna for creating the vessel or container within which I was able to grow and develop as an artist, do deep therapeutic work on myself, and be stimulated, encouraged and inspired by her guidance and the support of the others in the group."

Edna

On October 26, 2012 my mother fell and broke her hip. Little did I know at the time how this event would shape my life over the course of the next year. Every week I came to teach my long-standing weekly class of Expressive Kavannah bearing a heavy emotional load. My students suggested I take part in the sessions for my own therapy. They coaxed me to take advantage of the same opportunity I offered them to process my feelings in relation to my mother's worsening state. As an only child I felt all the burden on me. So, I readily accepted their suggestion to deal with my real life as the events unfolded.

However, I faced a true dilemma. How was I going to facilitate the group, hold the space for them and participate as well? I felt divided. I was distraught, and it was a relief not to hide my emotions. On the other hand, could I maintain my professionalism and focus to give to my students at the same time? I realized that I just had to be me. I knew I would feel comfortable sharing personally with this special group of people who had shared so much with me over the years. I had always witnessed their support for others in the group and confidentiality was an important aspect of our work together.

Considering the different modules of Expressive Kavannah, I realized that they were some I could easily participate in and remain available to them. We always started with journaling, so I also took advantage of this opportunity to update the last week's events. Following, as I joined in the free dancing which we do to feel the wisdom of our bodies, it felt so good to lighten my load. I taught my class as prepared, a psycho-spiritual interpretation of the week's Torah portion choosing relevant contemporary issues to be processed through meditation and image-making.

My own image-making was very intuitive and spontaneous. I produced quick brush strokes or collage that evoked my feelings at that time. I have included some of the images here as they became the genesis of the work in the studio.

Edna – "Sad, Mad, Glad" in class

At one point I realized that even these "quick paintings" were too involved to maintain my focus for the group, so I started an "image diary" with collages from magazines. Today, as I look back on the work I produced in the diary, I realize how fortunate I was to have had this context to record and process this trying time. It also gave me a chance to experience Expressive Kavannah in a very personal way and gain perspective on how it works for others through a deeply personal lens.

Edna – "Sad, Mad, Glad" print in studio

Adieu is a collection of etchings created in 2013-14 in response to my mother's death. Adieu, "farewell" and "to God" in French, reflects my mother's and my common language. The collection documents the deep and on-going mourning process that I expressed intuitively through my art of printmaking. The technique I used involves many processes, one of which is preparing printing plates. I intuitively "knew" that I wanted two equal plates divided in the middle, making a diptych to create a communication between two parallel plates divided by a gap. I strive to create in flow; I do not design or plan anything, rather let my soul guide me. I honor the fact that my artistic expressions quite often precede my intellectual understanding.

As I completed the first spontaneous piece I produced, "Hope", I understood that this creation was powerful and important, the beginning of a new phase in my psyche and consequently in my work. As I contemplated the piece, I felt how the pain in it related to my mother's death. This deep pain that was only the beginning of my process. Over the year, the powerful creations I produced came from a deep place of psychological and physical pain. The techniques

I chose to get the desired effects were difficult, and even dangerous. I often used very strong undiluted acid to cause the plate to disintegrate and decompose. I always used a mask to protect myself, but it was very debilitating to work that way. I described it as excruciating, but the process seemed to be part of what I had to experience, paralleling my mother's own long period of deterioration. The paradox is, that no matter how "arduous" the process was, I remained focused, absorbed and totally involved for art's sake, a state of mind Csikszentmihalyi describes brilliantly as Flow.

On the completion of the first work, my process of mourning was just beginning. The pieces together represented deep transformative experiences and revelations that preceded conscious knowing. I have learned to trust my intuition, the impetus for the spiritual creative process. I experience clarity and growth as a spiritual artist which in turn brought healing and insight into our lifelong mother-daughter relationship.

Edna —"Memories"

Edna —"Entwined"

EPILOGUE - GRATITUDE

Completion of this book has been my challenge for 20 years. Teaching concurrently, I started writing it first as a PhD thesis and then as an independent project. Finally, after I presented the Expressive Kavannah model at the 2013 IEATA conference, my mentor appeared and encouraged me to write a book. I am deeply indebted to the vision and faith of fellow artist and art therapist, Dr. Pat Allen. Her intuition that I had something very important to share, provided the stimulus I needed.

To verify Jewish content, I enlisted my dear friend Rabbi Elie Spitz who graciously offered both erudite and practical feedback. A special thanks to my dear friend and colleague Sally Klein-Katz who profoundly helped in the conceptualization and organization of the educational presentation and trusted me to teach her graduate Jewish education students at HUC.

From the time I decided to study expressive arts therapies at the European Graduate School, I want to acknowledge my many inspirational teachers both in Switzerland and in Israel, most notably Dr. Shaun McNiff.

As the book was starting to take shape, my husband David, a gifted writer, offered to edit it. This was a true blessing for me. David understands what I want to say and is able to get me to express it.

I am grateful for the abundant blessings of creativity that have enabled my artistic career to blossom and flourish. Together with my studies in education, expressive arts therapy and Jewish learning, my path led me to develop Expressive Kavannah. The methodology that I have presented in this book flows from my conviction that all humans are endowed with the capability to express themselves creatively and that those very acts can be of significant healing benefit psychologically and emotionally.

With humility I offer my own experience as a guide, just as so many others have done for me. I hope my fellow spiritual seekers, may find value in unlocking their own unique, innate creative impulses. My meditations and Jewish spiritual practices are my own, I do not seek to impose what works for me on others. I continue to travel a path beyond my self-centered domain to one embracing the age-old Jewish values of *kavannah*, focused intention, *mitzvah*, selfless act, and *tikkun olam*, repair of the world. Like many others, I seek a transformation rooted in encountering the unknown without fear and allowing godliness to work its magic in my life. Although my model is inspired and based on my Jewish tradition, I feel it carries a universal message.

GODLINESS

God.
Where?
Not in me nor in you
But between us.
God.
Not me or mine,
Not you or yours
But ours.
God.
Known
Not in isolation
But in relationship.
God.
In joy and in sorrow
In celebration and commemoration
In laughter and in tears
In despair and in hope.
God.
Covenanted.
Sacred claims, obligations, commandments
Above, below, between
Healing, binding, saving
Redeeming, shielding, nurturing

"Godliness *Elohut*"
Rabbi Harold M.Schulweis(*z"l*, of blessed memory)

Bibliography

Allen, Pat B. *Art is a Way of Knowing.* Shambhala Publications: Boston & London. 1995.

Art is a Spiritual Path. Shambhala Publications: Boston & London. 2005.

Allen, Pat B. & Allen, Adina. 'The Presence of What is Absent.' The Reform Jewish Quarterly, Winter, 2013.

Botero, Fernando. 'Online Quotes on Art'. www.art-quotes.com

Brooke, Avery. *Healing in the Landscape of Prayer.* Cowley Publications: Boston. 1996.

Buber, Martin. *I and Thou.* Charles Scribner's Sons: New York. 1958.

Cameron, Julia. *The Artist's Way.* Tarcher/Putnam Book: New York 1992.

Creative Teaching. www.creativeteachingsite.com

Caspi, Yair. *Inquiring of God: Foundations of Talmudic & Biblical Psychology.* Jerusalem. 1991.

Csikszentmihalyi, Mihaly. *Flow: The Psychology of Optimal Experience.* Harper Perennial Modern Classics: New York. 2008.

Creativity: Flow and the Psychology of Discovery and Invention. Harper Perennial Modern Classics: New York. 2009.

Frankel, Estelle. *Sacred Therapy: Jewish Spiritual Teachings on Emotional Healing and Inner Wholeness.* Shambhala: Boston & London. 2005.

Frankl, Victor. *Man's Search for Meaning.* Beacon Press: Boston. 1959.

Goleman, Daniel, Kaufman, Paul, and Ray, Michael. *The Creative Spirit.* Dutton Books: New York. 1992.

Green Arthur. *The Heart of the Matter: Studies in Jewish Mysticism and Theology.* The Jewish Publication Society: Philadelphia. 2015.

Heschel, Abraham J. *God in Search of Man: A Philosophy of Judaism.* Farrar, Straus & Giroux: New York. 1955.

Between God and Man: An Interpretation of Judaism. The Free Press: New York. 1959.

The Sabbath: Its Meaning for Modern Man. Noonday Press: New York. 1951.

Hoffman, Edward. *The Heavenly Ladder.* Harper Row Publishers: San Francisco. 1985.

Hoffman, Lawrence A. *My People's Prayer Book: The Sh'ma and its Blessings, Vol. 1.* Jewish Lights Publishing: Woodstock, Vermont. 1997.

Jung, C.G. *The Portable Jung.* Penguin Random House. 1976.

Kandinsky, Wassily. *Concerning the Spiritual in Art*. Dover Press: New York. 1977.

Kaplan, Aryeh. *Jewish Meditation – A Practical Guide.* Schocken Books: New York. 1985.

Knill, Paolo. *Minstrels of the Soul.* Palmerston Press: Toronto. 1995.

Kirschenbaum, Howard & Estate of Carl Rogers. *The Carl Rogers Reader*. Houghton Mifflin Co.: New York. 1989.

Landes, Daniel. *My People's Prayer Book: The Sh'ma and its Blessings, Vol 1.* Jewish Lights Publishing: Woodstock, Vermont. 1997.

LeShan, Lawrence. *How to Meditate.* Little, Brown & Company: Boston. 1974

Levine, Stephen, K. *Poesis: The Language of Psychology and the Speech of the Soul.* Palmerston Press: Toronto. 1992.

Lew, Alan. *This is Real and You are Completely Unprepared.* Little, Brown & Co.: Boston. 2011.

London, Peter *No More Second Hand Art: Awakening the Artist Within.* Shambhala Press: Boston & London. 1989.

Maisel, Eric. *Fearless Creating.* Tarcher/Putnam: New York. 1995.

Matt, Daniel. *God and the Big Bang.* Jewish Lights Publishing. 1996.
The Essential Kabbalah. Harper Collins Publishers: San Francisco. 1995.

May, Rollo. *The Courage to Create.* Bantam Books & W.W. Norton: New York. 1975.

Mayo Clinic (www.mayoclinic.org/healthylifestyle/stress/meditation)

McConeghey, Howard. *Art and Soul.* Putnam Spring Publications: Connecticut. 2003.

McNiff, Shaun. *Depth Psychology.* Charles C. Thomas Publishers: Springfield, Illinois. 1989.

Art as Medicine: Shambhala Publishers: Boston & London. 1992.

Earth Angels. Shambhala Publishers Boston & London. 1995.

Trust the Process. Shambhala Publishers: Boston & London. 1998.

Art Based Research: Jessica Kingsley Publishers: London & Philadelphia.1998.

Creating with Others. Boston and London: Shambhala Publishers. 2003.

Art Heals. Boston and London: Shambhala Publishers. 2004.

Milgrom, Jo. *Handmade Midrash.* Jewish Publication Society: Philadelphia, New York, Jerusalem. 1992.

MOMA Publications. 'Jackson Pollock: Interviews, Articles, Reviews'. 1999.

Morinis, Alan. *Climbing Jacob's Ladder.* Shambhala Publications: Boston. 2002.

Spitz, Elie. *Does the Soul Survive?* Jewish Lights Publishing: Woodstock, Vermont. 2000.

Increasing Wholeness. Jewish Lights Publishing: Woodstock, Vermont. 2015.

Schulweis, Harold. *For Those Who Can't Believe.* Harper Collins: New York. 1994.

Living our Legacy: From Prose to Poetry. The Schulweis Institute. 2015.

Telushkin, Joseph. *A Code of Jewish Ethics: Love Your Neighbor as Yourself.* Penguin Random House: New York. 2009.

Trugman, A.A. *Orchard of Delights.* Ohr Chadash Publications: Israel. 2011.

Tuchman, Maurice. *The Spiritual in Art - Hidden Meanings in Abstract Art.* Los Angeles County Museum of Art Publication: Los Angeles. 1989.

Waskow, Arthur I. *Seasons of our Joy.* Summit Books: New York. 1982.

Weiss, Avi. *The Open Siddur Project.* www.opensiddurproject.org

Made in the USA
San Bernardino, CA
19 February 2019